Top Horse Training Methods Explored

Anne Wilson

David & Charles

A DAVID & CHARLES BOOK

Photographs were supplied by the following:
p7 David & Charles/Kit Houghton (courtesy of Julian Marczak);
pp15, 19 Sylvia Loch; p32 David & Charles/Bob Atkins;
p44 David & Charles/Matthew Roberts; p61 www.ponyboy.com;
p74 Parelli horsemanship by Coco; p89 Monty & Pat Roberts Inc.;
p107 Sylvia Stanier LVO; p115 Linda Tellington-Jones; p123 Lionel Delevingne;
p127 Richard Lüst; p130 David & Charles/Bob Atkins
Line illustration on p68 courtesy of Sylvia Loch

First published in the UK in 2004

Copyright © Anne Wilson 2004

Distributed in North America
by F&W Publications, Inc.
4700 East Galbraith Road
Cincinnati, OH 45236
1-800-289-0963

Anne Wilson has asserted her right to be identified as author of this work in
accordance with the Copyright, Designs and Patents Act, 1988.

A catalogue record for this book is available from the British Library.

ISBN 0 7153 1776 8

Printed in Singapore by KHL
for David & Charles
Brunel House   Newton Abbot   Devon

Commissioning Editor: Jane Trollope
Copy Editor: Angela Bailey
Desk Editors: Shona Wallis/Sarah Martin
Production Controller: Jennifer Campbell

Visit our website at www.davidandcharles.co.uk

David & Charles books are available from all good bookshops; alternatively
you can contact our Orderline on (0)1626 334555 or write to us at
FREEPOST EX2110, David & Charles Direct, Newton Abbot, TQ12 4ZZ (no
stamp required UK mainland).

Contents

Preface and Acknowledgments

This book is the brainchild of Susan McBane, and the content was her idea in the beginning. We were going to write it together until other events overtook Susan's life and the task was passed to me. I feel I should point out to readers that the opinions expressed, particularly in the General Issues and Conclusions chapter, are entirely my own. While Susan and I are in agreement on broad-based classical principles, our opinions may vary slightly concerning some details. This is a natural and very healthy situation, given that we are both passionate about our horses, and no two people are exactly alike. The airing of thoughts, ideas and methods is what this book is all about. The required research and exploration of ideas has been interesting and enjoyable for both of us. No one should be complacent about their knowledge. It is always good to investigate other ideas and explore methods.

Both Susan and I should like to point out that the training methods described in this book are not necessarily our own. It has been my intention to describe, as accurately as possible, the ideas that I have gleaned from my research into these various methods. I must also point out that if readers wish to know more, they should read the appropriate books, view the videos and attend demonstrations for themselves. (Where appropriate, contact details and further information concerning books and videos are listed at the end of this book.)

I would like to thank all those trainers who so generously gave their time to take part in an interview for this book. It should also be noted here that there are a multitude of trainers and other methods that I have not covered. This is not because they are any the less important or valid, but simply a matter of time and space. There is scope for a follow-up. Please let me know if you would like one.

I could never have written this book without the help, guidance, encouragement and editing of Susan McBane. I am immensely grateful that she has been generous enough to share with me her many years of writing experience. I also owe a huge debt of gratitude to Sylvia Loch who has encouraged my writing over the past seven years, as well as enlightening me towards a better way of riding. Without her, I should never have dreamed of writing this book.

My thanks go to my son Tom and to Claire Barber for their IT support, to my husband John, and to Lesley Stack, Alison Kovarovic and James Thomson for their support. Last but not least, a big thank you is due to my copy editor, Angela Bailey, for her patience and diligence. My thanks also to the staff at David & Charles.

ANNE WILSON

Foreword

One of the most common remarks I hear, particularly when teaching, is that horse owners do not know who to believe or trust when looking for a teacher or trainer for themselves and their horses. There are so many different training philosophies, so many different schools of thought, so many different individuals all presenting their own ideas, that it is no wonder that even quite experienced owners are at a loss to know who to listen to.

There is such a variety of trainers now, using purportedly natural, horsemanship-methods (causing potential confusion – if they are all natural why aren't they all the same?), traditional and alternative methods of groundwork and riding, and so many magazines all publicizing these ideas that sorting them out has been a truly Herculean task for the author, classical trainer Anne Wilson.

It has been one of those tasks which, if you'd known how it was going to be in the first place, you'd never have started it, and she nearly gave up a few times. I know from all the late night phone calls! I hope the result makes her realise how worthwhile it has all been. Anne has done a brilliant job and I am happy to recommend the book as essential reading to all seriously involved horse people.

Unfortunately, experts, in any field, will never all agree. So I can't really reply to the complaint posed at the beginning of this foreword. What I *can* say is that if you're serious about horses, stick with it and keep learning all you can. Critically and objectively assess what you learn from different sources, use your common sense and try to check up on what you find or what people tell you.

I promise you that somewhere along the way it will all start to fall into place, and you will realise that there will *never* be a consensus of opinion on the best way to deal with horses. But you will come to your own beliefs and philosophies, your own policies and preferences – and when you do, don't shy off comparing them with other people's and always, always be prepared to learn more, even if it's what *not* to do, which is just as important as the other.

This book is a really excellent starting point. Can you imagine gathering all the great trainers, past and present, together? It will never happen in person, but you've got something just as good here in your hands. Yes, you might read conflicting approaches, but you will learn a lot. I hope you make the most of the book and enjoy it.

SUSAN MCBANE

Introduction

'The true horseman is never too proud to learn,
nor too narrow minded to listen'

Why Is This Book Needed Today?

From the earliest days in the evolution of the human race, man has made use of the horse. Initially, horses were hunted as a source of food and, to a lesser extent, clothing. Although horsemeat is still eaten today, by far the greatest use of the horse now is as a ridden animal. When first domesticated, horses were used as beasts of burden. From that role in life, they progressed to being ridden and driven. It was at this time that they played such a vital role in the advance of human civilization, changing the life of mankind irrevocably by enabling greater distances to be travelled than ever before. Agriculture – which in turn enabled the emergence of settled communities – was born out of the use of the horse as a draught animal (being faster and stronger than oxen). Although the horse's role in agriculture has now largely been overtaken by the tractor and combine harvester, this development is relatively recent. Horses also took mankind into battle, carrying warriors as well as pulling heavy gun carriages.

Had it not been for the trusty horse, the world would be a totally different place today. There is, perhaps, some inherent desire in many horse people to rekindle the feelings of their ancestors. Although the history of the horse is well known, it tends to be forgotten in the current race for trophies and rosettes, and the quest for good horsemanship. Those striving to achieve good horsemanship could do well to bear in mind the evolution and history of the horse, however, because their legacy has a major bearing on both the role of the horse today and the way in which it can be trained.

In my own case, both my parents were terrified of horses, but from the time I could speak I wanted to get close to them. Up until I was five years old, we lived in London, where our daily bread delivery came by horse and cart. Our bread deliverer was called Dolly. She knew every stop on her round, and the first part of it was done in double-quick time. Dolly couldn't wait to get to our house, where she climbed the pavement so that I could feed her titbits over the garden wall – to the horror of my mother who thought I would get my hand bitten off! A love of horses is something we are obviously born with or without – I later found out that I had a great uncle who was a fine horseman in the cavalry. Wherever it came from, I thank God for the gift of my love of horses.

'the history of the horse tends to be forgotten in the race for trophies and rosettes ...'

Riding is one of the fastest growing leisure activities in the UK today. To illustrate my point, there were 250,000 spectators at the 2002 Badminton Horse Trials, compared with 86,000 at the FA Cup Final in Cardiff the same year. When the Spanish Riding School visits the UK, usually every four years, tickets are normally sold out well in advance. I have seen even non-riders with tears of emotion in their eyes at the beautiful, moving, spectacle of the Lipizzaner stallions performing their 'art in motion'. Horses seem to have a special place in people's hearts, and have the ability to touch the emotions of so many of us, even those who know nothing about them.

As a freelance trainer travelling to various locations, I see increasing numbers of completely novice riders keeping their own horses in livery yards. Over the past few years, many equestrian centres have closed owing to Government legislation and taxes on riding schools. If a keen rider finds it impossible to acquire lessons at a good school, then obviously the only path left for them is to buy their own horse, keep it at livery and employ the services of an instructor, when they can afford it. However, taking total responsibility for riding and looking after your own horse is a world apart from learning gradually at a good school.

'the enjoyment of achievement is just as real for the horse as for the rider...'

These keen horse lovers are often overzealous to do the right thing for their horses, and when they hear of a 'new' horse training method that purports to be easier, kinder and more natural, they often 'jump in with both feet'. The outcome is not necessarily bad, but there is the potential for things to go wrong if the new owner does not fully understand either the wider picture or the possible alternatives. We have lost so many of our old horsemen – the old-fashioned 'nagsmen' of the past, who understood so much about horses and who passed on their knowledge by word of mouth. In many livery yards today, someone who has been involved with horses for perhaps only five years may be considered to be experienced, and that person may be giving advice to the new owners on the yard.

I do not consider all the old practices in horse management to be good, and neither are all the new ones neccessarily bad. Veterinary science and modern inventions have enabled us to advance in many ways, helping us to give our horses longer, more comfortable lives. Surely what we should strive for is to keep the best of the old while utilizing the best of the new. It is, however, a source of regret that we are in danger of losing much of the 'instinctive' knowledge that the old 'nagsmen' seemed to possess, such as looking at a horse and knowing that it has a back problem. Imagine this type of instinctive 'feel' and empathy with the horse, backed up by modern science!

It is to try to unravel some of the mystique and contradictions in the equestrian world with which the new owner is faced that this book has been written. Some of my pupils have described their quest for knowledge as a feeling of being lost in a maze, and, without some form of guidance, they do not know which way to turn. Some horses today seem to be regarded by their owners/trainers merely as a piece of sports equipment, but I prefer to think of them primarily as companion/riding creatures, taking part in competition from time to time.

It is in the sphere of competition where things seem most likely to go wrong from the horse's point of view – not that there is anything at all wrong with competition in itself; quite the reverse. It should be fun, both for the participant and the spectator. It should give rise to better riding and horsemanship and encourage both horses and people to improve and have a feeling of achievement. The enjoyment of achievement, I believe, is just as real for the horse as for the rider, but problems arise when the goal of winning becomes more important than how it is achieved.

Unravelling the Details of the Available Techniques

The purpose of this book is to unravel some of the hitherto misunderstood and hard-to-fathom details of the many varying techniques available to us today. Sometimes the equestrian world can be very contradictory and confusing, particularly to new horse owners.

Although there are instances where I clearly state my views on an issue, I must emphasize that this book is a genuine attempt to describe and compare many differing equestrian training techniques in use today. The opinions, methods, ideas and philosophies described here are not necessarily either mine or those of the publisher. Also, where I have given my own interpretation and opinions, they are just that – my own. They are not necessarily those of other trainers, classical or otherwise.

Conversive Evolution

Where comparisons have been made and methods found to be similar, this is not to imply that the ideas have been 'taken' or 'copied', from one trainer to another. Although there is nothing wrong in using good training techniques and adapting them within one's own training system, it is not necessarily the case that this has happened. Good (and bad for that matter) ideas can be born independently. The evolutionary scientists call this 'conversive evolution' – where the same evolution is happening independently on different sides of the world. This premise is very clearly shown in the chapter discussing the horsemanship of the Native American Indians. The Native Americans came up with a very similar philosophy to that of the classical masters in their ways of handling and dealing with their horses. This must have happened at a time in history when they had no use for books, thus could not read, and had hardly any contact with the outside world. Therefore, when I find that methods are similar, it is not meant as a criticism, but merely an observation. In addition, methods that may be based, at least in part, on existing techniques are also to be welcomed if they can be of benefit to the horse and rider.

'the equestrian world can be contradictory and confusing …'

The chapters are not arranged in order of authority of trainers, and no extra importance is intended towards any particular person or training method. Where appropriate, I have included an interview with the trainer whose work I have described, although this was unfortunately not possible with the work of Linda Tellington-Jones, GaWaNi Pony Boy or Pat Parelli. A short description of the Feldenkrais method is included after the chapter on Linda Tellington-Jones, as she draws heavily on the Feldenkrais method for her work. A brief explanation of the sport of Doma Vaquera follows. In some instances, I have merely interviewed the trainer, without a full description of their work. In the case of Sylvia Loch and Sylvia Stanier, this is because their methods are very classical, and it would take a large book in itself to begin to describe them. Both of these trainers have excellent books of their own on the market, and it is not within the scope of this book to fully describe classical techniques.

'beauty and grace can never be hurried; it takes time to nurture'

In the field of international dressage, there have been some truly wonderful classical riders such as Reiner Klimke. His success in international dressage is very well known, and his horses went on winning year after year; the good old classical principles keeping them sound. The same goes for Mary King in the world of eventing. Classical riding is not just about dressage, but is the grounding for all disciplines. The rider can still be in balance and harmony with the horse when riding over fences.

Blurring of the Classical Principles

So why have people strayed from the tried and tested classical principles? Why do we see so many dressage riders today training their horses in draw reins and pulling the horse's head in towards its chest? The Fédération Equestre Internationale (FEI) clearly states in its rules for dressage that the horse's poll should be the highest point, and the nose should be just in front of the vertical. These are the rules by which our dressage judges are supposedly judging the competitions. Yet we see countless overbent horses, with noses pulled in towards the chest, and thus unable to take any appreciable weight back onto the haunches to lighten the forehand – and many of them still win competitions.

Why do we not see more people trying to emulate Reiner Klimke? My guess is impatience – it takes many years to train a dressage horse correctly. Money also plays a large part in the reasoning for these transgressions. People who have spent a large sum of money on acquiring a well-bred young horse want to see results sooner rather than later. I dare say this blurring of the classical principles has taken place over several years, and it would seem that gradually many of the judges have forgotten the rules, despite the fact that they are still readily available verbally and in print!

However, beauty and grace can never be hurried; it takes time to nurture. If the horse is forced to perform certain movements too soon, or forced into an 'outline' or 'frame' before he is ready, then the movement and paces become no more than robotic. The poor horse also pays a high price in terms of physical and mental well-being. Over a period of time, the robotically-performed movement becomes the 'norm', and spectators, as well as some judges, no longer seem to notice the lack of beauty and expression in the horse's paces – much less the lack of harmony between horse and rider.

It must be said here that this is not always the case. There are, thankfully, still some classical competitive riders today. However, there are far too many who are definitely not in that category, and yet they are still highly respected (by those who know no better) and are successful. Their horses, however, are far less likely to be happy and are highly likely to suffer injuries. Their life expectancy will be far lower than that of their classically-trained counterparts because of the undue strain on joints, ligaments, tendons and so on. Steady and methodical classical training has been proven, throughout the centuries, to actually strengthen the horse and make him much less prone to injury, enabling him to live a longer and more active life.

In my childhood days, the Pony Club, together with most traditional training schools in the UK, employed teaching methods that appeared to be very much more classically orientated than they are today. I can remember the British Horse Society (BHS)/Pony Club manual describing many classical movements, such as pirouettes. Sadly, the parameters seem to have changed over the years; the manual has been re-written several times, and these classical references have been reduced.

Influence of the Military

Most centres of excellence for equestrian instruction in the 1950s and 1960s were heavily influenced by the military, which in turn was greatly influenced by the classical masters. This too, has changed in more recent years.

I remember attending an excellent riding school during the late 1960s/early 1970s, which was run by an ex-cavalry officer. The standard of instruction was high and moderately classical, although it was not called classical. The horses too, were in tip-top condition; they were so fit that no pupil was allowed to go out on a hack until they could jump three foot (1m) without reins or stirrups. The basis for this was that if you were able to stay on over the jump, then your balance was good enough to stay on, no matter what happened out on a hack. Looking back, I think that this regime was very harsh, although I fully appreciate the importance placed upon the balance of the rider. I am sure that it was this school which 'saved my skin' in many situations in later life, when I would doubtless otherwise have fallen off. Very little emphasis was put upon 'getting the horse on the bit' as is so common nowadays. The emphasis was on an independent seat and quiet hands. The horse's roundness was something that came when his stage of training and physique allowed.

'the emphasis was on an independent seat and quiet hands'

Nevertheless, I prefer to teach in a more gentle way and to make it an enjoyable experience for horse and rider, while still emphasizing the importance of a balanced seat and the ability to ride without relying on reins or stirrups. I am often appalled today at the practice of allowing beginners to canter for the first time while holding the reins. It is almost inevitable that they will use them for their own balance. I will never allow people to take up the reins in trot or canter until they have demonstrated an independent seat. This, of course, requires many lessons initially on the lunge, but if that is what it takes, then so be it.

The Dangers of Competition

Sadly, it seems that many people have become more influenced by what has developed into 'the competition style of dressage'. The classical principles seem to become altered when serious competition enters the equation. Winning is often the only aim, and the process of how one gets there is inconsequential. If only people realised that winning under these circumstances completely nullifies the meaning of the prize. To my mind, they may as well go out and buy themselves a championship cup!

Nevertheless, there are still pockets of classical horsemanship being kept alive, and even growing, all over the world today. Maybe it is the confusion over what appear to be different 'styles' of riding that has contributed to the popularity of new training techniques. People are actually trying to get back the feeling of closeness with their horses. This has to be applauded, but we must be careful not to jump in with both feet without first testing the water. That is really what I set out to do in this book.

Alternative Training Methods: Xenophon Revitalized?

Over the past decade or so, a myriad of new training techniques has become popular in the equestrian world. The first that springs to mind is Monty Roberts and his join-up technique. This is a method to be welcomed, in as much as it is clearly a preferable way of preparing a young horse to be backed, compared with the barbaric methods hitherto used by his father's generation in that part of America, but this is just by comparison. We do have to look further than this simplistic comparison if we are to understand and come closer to perfect harmony with our equine companions. Fans of Monty Roberts or Pat Parelli can be assured that we are not out to discredit alternative training methods in any way. Rather, the aim of this book is to discuss the pros and cons – the similarities and differences – of alternative training methods compared with the classical principles.

'…these approaches, while claiming to be new discoveries, are in fact old techniques'

It is also possible that the changing role of horses in our society today has engendered a recent upsurge in new training techniques. Many of these approaches, while claiming to be new discoveries, are in fact old techniques, (employed by classical training masters through the ages), revamped and called by different names. What may, in fact, be a reinvention should be applauded rather than denounced, however, if it serves to bring good methods – perhaps in a more understandable format – to the attention of those who may not otherwise have considered them.

Throughout the ages, many people have chosen to ignore the advice of such classical riding masters as Xenophon, who wrote *The Art of Horsemanship* (JA Allen 1962) in approximately 400BC. Xenophon advocated a kind and fair regime for the training of horses, but this seems to have been repeatedly forgotten or ignored throughout the centuries. Horrendous practices such as hobbling or physically restraining horses, who are terrified until there is no fight left in them, have arisen.

True Horsemen: Never Too Proud to Learn

When these cruel practices become the 'norm' in a region, good-hearted people who want to improve the horse's lot in life are prompted to invent new training techniques. When reviewing any horse-training technique it is, of course, vital to sift out the 'good' from the 'bad' methods. It is also important, however, that we do not discard any new ideas that may benefit our horses and us – even if some of those ideas are based on philosophies of a bygone era that may have become largely forgotten over time. All people and all horses are different, and the true horseman is never too proud to learn, nor too narrow minded to listen!

CHAPTER 1

Summary of Classical Principles

'Classical riding is not elitist – it is just correct riding.
It is the orginal 'natural' system'

C lassical riding has been kept alive and the ethos and methods passed down through the centuries by word of mouth as well as in the books written by the great riding masters. Some of the most famous of these classical riding academies are as follows (although this list is not definitive):

- The Spanish Riding School in Vienna, Austria
- The French School at Saumur, France
- Le Cadre Noir at Saumur (the elite of the French School), France
- The Portuguese School of Equestrian Art in Queluz, Portugal
- The Royal Andalusian School of Equestrian Art in Jerez, Spain

As mentioned previously, our first written word on classical horsemanship came from Xenophon in approximately 400BC. Since then, there have been many great riding masters. Some of their ideas and practices have differed slightly, but all have the same basic classical principles.

'a good war horse was a really prized possession'

In Xenophon's day, it is obvious from his book, that a good war horse was a really prized possession. The movements and exercises of dressage were first devised for purposes of war, the object being to increase the flexibility and balance of the horse, thereby rendering him faster and more manoeuvrable. The famous 'airs above the ground' were taken from the horse's natural movements and enlarged upon for the benefit of the warrior. For instance, the levade – a controlled rear where the horse sits back on his haunches, balancing over his back legs (which are tucked well underneath him), lifting his front legs and forehand – could take a warrior quickly away from an advancing blow. The capriole, where the horse leaps into the air, thrusting both back legs out behind him, could be quite damaging to an enemy approaching from behind.

Maybe it is the fact that soldiers no longer actually do battle on horseback that has caused these advanced movements to be very rarely practised today, other than in the schools of highest excellence such as the Spanish Riding School. In addition, of course, the degree of difficulty and level of training required by horse and rider may well have much to do with their omission from general dressage tests. However, it is this ultimate balance and ability to lighten the forehand that is the aim of all dressage exercises.

No classical dressage movements are unnatural; they are all movements that the horse will perform happily on his own when free. The skill arises when he is asked to recapture this balance and agility while carrying the extra weight of the rider. However, with many years of painstaking, patient work, most horses can achieve a fairly high degree of lightness and balance, regardless of their type or breeding. Of course you do not have to have such high aims. Whatever level you are aiming for, even hacking around the countryside, you and your horse will benefit from the very basic classical principles. You can learn the basics without ever getting as far as lateral movements if that is your wish.

There have been outstanding masters such as the Frenchman Francois Robichon de la Guérinière, who invented the shoulder-in as we know it today, and the Englishman William Cavendish, Duke of Newcastle. Guérinière's approach, however, was altogether more gentle and therefore, in my opinion, more classical. The history of classical horsemanship is well documented, and although there have been disagreements on certain points throughout the centuries, the basics have remained the same.

Classical horsemanship is not merely confined to riding but encompasses everything to do with horses and, in fact, should affect our whole outlook on life. To be a really good classical horseman, you must foster all the best character traits such as love, humility, patience, kindness, empathy, a sense of justice, self discipline and so on. If you do not foster these attributes, then you are very likely to fall by the wayside sometime on your equestrian journey. The road to true harmony with the horse, although wonderfully uplifting and rewarding, also takes courage, stoicism and determination. Thus, the desire to win trophies should pale into insignificance compared with the joy of training our horses correctly, regardless of which discipline we decide to follow.

'true harmony with the horse takes courage, stoicism and determination'

A Good Foundation for Everyday Riders

Many people think of classical riding as elitist, difficult, or just 'posh'. Nothing could be further from the truth – it is just correct riding. In fact, it is the original 'natural' system. Natural because it follows the laws of nature, gravity and balance.

For instance, to turn the horse, say, to the right in walk, if you put a little extra weight into your right stirrup, advance your right hip, let your left leg slide slightly back and turn your shoulders to the right, the horse will turn right. Excluding horses who are spooking, napping and/or in pain, every horse will respond to this natural aid, with no need for training or turning with the reins. If the rider's body position is held, then a circle should be the result. It is in this way that the reins can become a means of more subtle communication between horse and rider. All that is needed to ask the horse to flex his head and neck to the right should be a closing of the fingers around the reins – no need for any pulling. Of course when horse and rider become finely attuned to these natural aids, then the aids can become virtually invisible.

These aids are literally that: they 'aid' or help the horse to do what is required. They are not a system of instructions. The way it works is quite simple. The most comfortable way for the horse to carry his rider is for the rider to sit upright, taking responsibility for their own weight. If the rider's weight moves slightly to one side, the most comfortable thing for the horse to do, in order to stay in balance, is to move under the weight.

When riding a turn or a circle, the inside hip needs to be in advance of the outside one. The smaller the circle, the more the inside hip needs to advance. Just try walking a small-circle on foot with your hands on your hips, and you will feel how your inside leg naturally carries a little more weight and your inside hip is in advance of the outside one. This is how it should be ridden. It gives the horse the best chance to perform a correct and comfortable circle, mirroring the rider's position. Just to prove the point, try walking a circle on foot, slightly weighting your outside leg, and see how difficult it is – try not to fall over.

There are also ways of halting or slowing the horse without touching the reins, using similar natural aids. This way of riding allows the use of the rein contact to become one of fine-tuning and support for the horse. Riding without reins in anything other than a walk should, in my opinion, be reserved for only a highly schooled horse who is able to hold himself in self-carriage, without the need for support from the rider. The picture of classical riders performing beautiful exercises with reins in loops can only be achieved after years of work. In the early stages, the horse is reliant on the support from the rider, but that is not at all the same as the rider 'pulling' on the reins.

A Good Foundation for All Disciplines

The above examples are a simplification of a complex subject, but I hope that readers will understand that these principles are not elitist, nor beyond the capabilities of everyday riders. The application of these classical aids, combined with a classical seat, is of immense value to every rider, whether you want to ride a dressage test, participate in eventing competitions, or just hack around the countryside. The following are just a few of the important reasons why classical training should form the basis of everyone's equestrian curriculum, regardless of which particular training method – or perhaps elements of different methods – they then choose to adopt:

1 Horse and rider will be more comfortable, forming a harmonious relationship.
2 The rider will be safer, having a more secure seat and more able to stay in balance with the horse in times of disunity, such as if the horse shies or trips.
3 The horse should learn to take more weight onto the haunches, lightening the forehand, which greatly enhances the chances of the horse staying sound and probably living longer, staving off the effects of arthritis.
4 The horse-and-rider combination will be more effective, greatly enhancing the chances of success in any discipline of competition. For instance, a show jumping horse-and-rider combination who are in balance and harmony will be faster around corners, and their approach to fences will be more balanced, giving them a much better chance to win!

This is obviously a brief description of classical principles and ethos. There are many excellent books available on this subject (see page 142). I hope this has aroused your interest.

CHAPTER 2

Sylvia Loch

Classical Riding in the Context of Horse Welfare

*'The only thing I get worried about is the
'emperor's new clothes' syndrome. So often, people
claim to have invented a new and natural method
and this is absolute nonsense'*

ylvia Loch is very well known to many horse-minded people all over the world. Her books and videos sell like hot cakes in the USA as well as in the UK, and two major books have been translated into French and German. Many readers will already be acquainted with her work. However, many people may not be aware of the extent of her knowledge and her truly international background. I will not try to recount Sylvia's entire equestrian life story – which would be a hard task even if given the space of a book in itself – but rather to give a short resumé.

Sylvia learned to ride at an early age, and, by the time she was only 14 years old, people were beginning to bring difficult ponies to her for training. She continued schooling difficult horses until she was about 20. During this time, she was involved in many equestrian sports, from Pony Club camps to event riding. During her twenties, Sylvia travelled a great deal and witnessed the horsemanship of many countries, including South America. She finally settled in Portugal where she met and married ex-cavalry officer Lord Henry Loch, 29 years her senior.

Henry Loch had trained before the war at Weedon Cavalry School before going to Sandhurst and being commissioned into the 11th Hussars. Weedon was a traditional English Army school where classical principles were very much to the fore. Students were given the opportunity to visit the Spanish Riding School in Vienna as well as the French classical school at Saumur.

'based on a strong Portuguese and French influence – 'lightness' was the key word'

It was in Portugal that Sylvia was introduced to high school horses and riding. She saw, at first hand, the proud and effortless way in which most of the Portuguese rode their horses, the way in which the horses carried themselves, and the obvious harmony between horse and rider. She began to learn the true art of classical riding from Henry, as well as from her observations of many great riders in Portugal. During the ten years that Sylvia lived in Portugal, their small dressage school (which was started by Henry Loch) expanded and attracted students from all over the world. Henry did most of the teaching at this time, while Sylvia did the schooling and administration.

In late 1979, Sylvia and Henry were persuaded by their many students to move back to the UK, bringing with them their beautiful Lusitano horses and their methods, based on a strong Portuguese and French influence; 'lightness' was the key word. At Henry's family home in Suffolk, they set up the first Iberian classical school of equitation and Lusitano stud in Britain, and Sylvia was the founder of the Lusitano Breed Society of Great Britain.

With Henry's sudden death in 1982, it was, very sadly, financially necessary for the main body of the stud to be disbursed. However, Sylvia continued to teach with her remaining horses and gave countless clinics, lectures and demonstrations in the UK as well as in other countries, including Australia, New Zealand, South Africa, Kenya and the USA.

Over the years, Sylvia has done much academic research, enabling her to combine the physical side of riding with the academic and philosophical aspects. Much of this research has been influenced by her friendships with Kurt Albrecht (former Director of the Spanish Riding School), Eva Podhajsky (wife of the late Colonel Alois Podhajsky), Michel Henriquet (a world authority on classical riding), and Nuño Oliveira. She is also a life member of the Teaching the Trainers of Tomorrow Trust. All of this has no doubt combined to make her magazine articles and books so popular throughout the world. Her regular column in *Horse and Rider* magazine is well known, and over the past two decades she has written six books.

In 1995, Sylvia started the Classical Riding Club, a non-profit-making club, dedicated to the continuance and promotion of the principles of classical equitation. Students, riders and trainers, as well as non-riding horse-lovers can all benefit from exchanging ideas, supporting each other, and furthering their learning of this most wonderful and uplifting art.

> *'riders and trainers, as well as non-riding horse-lovers, can all benefit from exchanging ideas...'*

QUESTION 1: *I know that one of the reasons you started the Classical Riding Club in 1995, as a non-profit-making club, was to improve the welfare of horses in general and, in particular, sport horses. We must all be familiar with the sight of over-bent horses (noses pulled behind the vertical, back towards the horse's chest). During the past 20 years or so in the UK, and elsewhere, a large number of trainers seem to pay scant regard to the need to allow the horse time to develop the muscles of the top body line, as well as the hindquarters. The latter has a major effect on the subsequent strength and flexibility in the joints of the hind limbs. Do you see this now gradually changing as people are willing to explore and understand the principles of classical riding?*

SYLVIA'S REPLY: I did indeed start the Classical Riding Club as a response to what I saw as misguided methods used in training. It concerned me that many people were not familiar with the bio-mechanics of the horse, or indeed the correct muscle development, and therefore their training methods were based on what they perceived to be a correct outline. I do not blame people for these misconceptions, because all of us had to start somewhere, and I wish that when I was a young person, I had understood more about the horse's bio-mechanics and both his physical and mental development.

However, in those days, horses were not expected to be in an 'outline' as such. Since there was very little dressage, except as a part of the system within eventing, to prepare the horse and make him softer and lighter for when he went jumping, there was less damage being done by riders; they simply assumed that the horse was a horse, and that concepts like 'coming onto the bit' would arise only when the horse was ready for it. Since people's expectations were less demanding, you would not get marked down in a basic-level dressage test if your horse was not completely on the bit. It was very much that the horse should be light on the hands, forward-going, and the outline was very much left to how the horse was to develop, rather than that he had to be in a certain shape by a certain age. In this way, horses were not damaged so much by their riders, in that nothing was forced, stretched or stressed, too early on.

I think that the danger nowadays is that not everyone is willing to explore and understand the principles of classical riding. Many riding schools do not place enough importance on the 'whys' and 'wherefores' behind the end result. Therefore people get the wrong idea; they think that they have to have a horse looking like a million dollars within the first few months of training. This should of course comprise the end result, but it is not explained how to get there or how it is to develop naturally with correct training methods. You cannot just fix the horse's head into position and expect the neck to develop lovely big top-line muscles without putting in the groundwork.

Yes, there are people taking the trouble to learn the correct ways, but not enough! I think that it is helping enormously that there are more and more people out there, not just myself, speaking up for the horse and explaining that training methods must never be rushed. The problem factor is still very much that the outline is something that happens because the rider demands it, rather than the fact that the horse is ready for it. It is a question, to which I cannot really give a positive answer, and probably never will, until everyone is familiar with these practices. At this moment in time, not everyone is – not even everyone in dressage.

QUESTION 2: *Why do you think that so many people have no understanding of simple weight aids, which seem so natural to a true classical rider?*

SYLVIA'S REPLY: The reason I think that a lot of people have no understanding of simple weight aids is that many people do not ride out across country any more. When one learns as a child to walk, trot, canter and gallop, over open countryside, one naturally learns to distribute weight in a way that would make things easy for the horse. You do this out of sheer self-preservation, if nothing else.

'the outline should happen when the horse is ready – not because the rider demands it'

For example, I will never forget going in a pretty fast canter around a corner with two slightly more inexperienced riders in front of me, and I could see the accident coming before it happened. The rider immediately in front was leaning the wrong way and instead of moving into the movement with her horse and supporting it to the inside by staying very central and very quiet, she collapsed to the inside and her shoulders went to the outside. The horse fell over, simply because the weight was so unbalanced. I think that this was perhaps the first time that I really was aware of the importance of weight, although, as I said, it was something which had developed instinctively.

Today many people do not have the chance to ride out, and there are many people who ride dressage or work in the school who have never actually ridden a horse in full gallop. If they had, they would be much more aware of the importance of weight, just as a good jockey is. It does not really matter whether we are riding the Aintree course or riding in a school, the horse still needs us to be in harmony with him, and weight aids are extremely important. They form the whole crux of good riding. You would not send a boat out to sea which was incorrectly weighted, or an aeroplane into the sky which was incorrectly weighted, because without the balance being correct you can risk a horrible accident. Every time we ride a horse, we really have to make ourselves aware that we have the same responsibility to him with our weight. Again it is a message that is slow to get through, because it is almost something that has gone out of the nation's subconscious.

I think people are less close to their horses; they live in a more artificial environment, and, for those who keep their horse at livery, they do not even have the chance always to observe them at liberty in the field – so it is no-one's fault. It is basically just the general modern scene, that people are less close to their horse, less close to being able to move with him freely over changing and difficult terrain, and therefore not getting the experience of feel that is so necessary in order for a rider to learn the importance of weight and how it affects balance. When it comes to having dressage lessons, it always seems strange and new, when in fact it should be in the rider's subconscious.

QUESTION 3: *Having lived in Portugal for a number of years, do you think that there is a great difference in the attitude towards equine welfare in the UK where you currently live as opposed to, say, Portugal?*

SYLVIA'S REPLY: I have not only lived in Portugal, and I have also travelled a great deal, so my answer to this question will not necessarily be based on Portugal. I have spent time in South America, South Africa, Australia, New Zealand and so on. I have also taught in Australasia, Kenya, North America, and in several countries within the European Union.

I think that in the UK, we have a fantastic history of equine welfare, and I think that for many years we have led the way as regards stable care, turnout, correct rugging, bandaging, feeding and so on. Of course in the UK, we are blessed too by the fact that we have a wonderful agricultural heritage, where good cereals, good hay and straw have been provided for at least the past two centuries, and it is a horseman's paradise when it comes to grass and natural foraging.

In hot countries, it is impossible to keep horses in the same way unless you are well off enough to be able to afford the artificial watering of fields and paddocks. The amount of grazing that can be provided for horses is very limited and normally just in certain months of the year – in Portugal, for example, from February to April was about it, in so far as our small farm in the Algarve was concerned. We could not afford irrigation because we did not have the water. In fact, we had to buy water for our house, so that gives you an idea of how lucky we are in the UK with constant rainfall throughout the year. Because of the lack of water in other countries, horses are often kept in what one might call very artificial environments, ie they have to be stabled and some will never be turned out in their lives.

This can be managed kindly, although there will always be those who argue that it cannot. However, I have truly seen many, many horses that are contented and happy to live in a box, or even a stall, provided the rest of the management is correct. I always remember lines and lines of stallions in both Portugal and Spain in the early 1960s, where the only exercise given was the riding, but they were so happy and satisfied with their riding turnouts that it did not appear to worry the majority of stallions that they were not turned out to graze.

'I was shocked to see yards where horses are left without water for hours on end ...'

As regards other matters such as bandaging or protective clothing, again in hot countries people tend not to use these as much because of the heat. Often bandaging can make horse's legs very sweaty, and this can lead to other problems. Rugs are often unnecessary. I think basically that this allows people to perhaps be a little lax over certain other things. In the better yards, which tend to be where people are employed and everyone has their job to do, feeding hours and matters of routine are very much by the clock. However, in yards of only one or two horses where it is the owner looking after them, matters may be very different. I have often been shocked in some yards in the world where horses are left without water for hours on end, where the horses are plagued with flies, and only when the owner gets back from work, or from being away, are they fed and watered. This seems to me unnecessarily cruel, but unfortunately to others it is not perceived as such. Of course, there are many owners who go out to work and 'do' their own horses, and the animals are catered for admirably. It is a matter of organization and making provision for the horses when the owner cannot be there. That is where education becomes so important.

In many countries, animals do not come first; people come a long way up the charts. I have been to yards where I have seen children teasing, and even hitting, horses, and in one case firing make-believe shots from a model Sten gun, and there have been adults present who have said nothing. They think it is quite amusing – in other words, the child is more important than the horse, and the child will not be reprimanded for treating the horse as an object rather than as a living creature. In the same country, I have seen the complete opposite, so one cannot make sweeping judgements. I still maintain that, as a race, we tend to have a great love for all animals. It can be argued that perhaps equine welfare is at its highest in the UK, but I have to say that this does not necessarily bear true as regards the training methods we use.

My biggest concern is that there is now a huge disparity in riding techniques, so one person is teaching one thing, another teaching another, and so on. At least on the European continent, there appears to be a much more uniform method of teaching riding, and since the riding of the horse does come into welfare, you could argue that the welfare is improved because of that. It is a difficult one.

QUESTION 4: *In your capacity as a judge and trainer in the USA, do you find the standard of equine welfare, as well as the standard and style of riding, different from elsewhere?*

SYLVIA'S REPLY: This too is difficult because again there are several different ways of riding in the USA, just as there are beginning to be in the UK. There is quite a difference from the Western approach and, obviously, the hunter/jumper approach, which is based on British equestrianism. Then there are the gaited horses, and in certain areas you have a more Spanish outlook, influenced by the Mexicans and the South Americans. It very much depends on whereabouts you are in the USA. In a very general way, it is very much that the British influence exists on the east coast, and, of course, as you will know, they still have fox-hunting in North America.

The Americans have always liked a barn arrangement for stabling their horses, and I think that this is great, because the horses can see each other and there is a nice presence of people around generally and plenty to keep the horses' minds occupied. I do, however, think that horses also need peace. One of the things against the barn arrangement, I believe, is that nowadays people are doing a lot of competing and shifting their horses over large areas, and this would apply even more in the USA than in the UK. You can go to a show, and it can take a day or two days to get there. People are often coming in and out throughout the night, or getting up very early in the morning to get horses ready, and I suppose when you have a barn arrangement, this can be quite disturbing.

I have a strong feeling that horses should be quiet for some periods of each day, and it would be natural and nice if their sleep could be fairly uninterrupted. I know that when on the occasions that I go to shows, the other horses are quite resentful at being woken up and can be quite grumpy the next day, just like people. However, in large livery yards with a barn system this is unavoidable, so if one person is coming in and disturbing their horse, all the horses are going to be disturbed. I guess nothing is ever ideal.

I find that, as in the UK, the Americans have a great love of their horses. Generally, I would say that the standard and style of riding is similar to ours, except in those areas where there is no hacking and the greater distances prevent people from being able to find trainers of worth. I do get a lot of letters from people in the USA and Canada, saying that they live too far away from any good trainer to have any help, and this is perhaps where books and videos are so important. In fact I believe that our Classical Riding Club newsletter has made a huge difference to people living in outlying areas of America, where it may mean travelling your horse for over 600 miles to get to the nearest trainer.

QUESTION 5: *What do you think of Western riding?*

SYLVIA'S REPLY: I think, as with anything, good Western riding can be superb and is very attractive. I see it as doing no harm to the horse whatsoever and is not so different from classical riding if the correct principles are employed. What I dislike is when all these things become 'faddish' and people go out of their way to make them different. I have been horrified to see some riders allow, even encourage, their horses to slop along with their head between their knees, in what can only be called an abusive mode of riding. Sadly, a lack of knowledge lulls these riders into thinking that what they are doing is acceptable. Often it is the 'mode' and demanded in certain show rings, but bio-mechanically it is so damaging for the horse.

'a lack of knowledge lulls riders into thinking that what they are doing is acceptable'

Then there are those riders who exaggerate a Western 'position'. They have an over-long stirrup and end up at the back of the saddle instead of in the middle and think that this is good. Sometimes their idea of a light hand on the rein becomes a rein that allows the horse to be completely disconnected.

Then there is the opposite scenario, where people who have no control of their hands use horrendous curbs in their horses' mouths and have no idea of the powerful effect it exerts on the horses' jaw and poll. I hate polarization in riding. I think that all good riding should have the same principles, whether it is racing, jumping, flatwork or western riding. A good western rider for me is just as much of a pleasure to watch as anyone.

QUESTION 6: *What do you think of the sport of Doma Vaquera?*

SYLVIA'S REPLY: I would say that the same can be said of the sport of Doma Vaquera. In Spain, the natural home of this discipline, the riding out in the countryside can be absolutely stunning and immaculate.

A good Doma Vaquera rider is so much at one with his horse, moving him with just the slightest pressure of the knee or thigh. He sits like a statue, and together they represent a fantastic picture. A bad Doma Vaquera is as unattractive to me as a bad dressage rider, a bad hunting rider, or a bad show jumper. Doma Vaquera should not involve anything other really than the classical principles of being able to move the horse easily with tiny aids – mainly body and pressure of the legs, hardly a touch on the rein (since the horse should be in a very well-balanced state). There should exist an almost mental telepathy between horse and rider. That is what I have seen in both Portugal and Spain out on the range with what I call good natural horsemen.

In Portugal, we call the men who work the cattle with horses 'Campinos'. Indeed my late husband and I often used to buy horses for our school that had been used by Campinos and often found them very sensitive and obedient. On the other hand, there was the odd one with a mouth like steel, because the rider was less educated and had abused the horse's mouth with a very strong curb. Again, all this is relative; good Doma Vaquera riders, as I have said, can be absolutely wonderful, but the opposite, of course, can also be true in certain cases. I think that this is what happens when this sport is perhaps introduced artificially and exploited by people who really have no knowledge of how it originated or where it developed. To my mind, Doma Vaquera is something that is done actively with the cattle over open countryside, testing horse and man in the art of moving cattle over very large distances.

QUESTION 7: *Do you think that the current trend towards new trainers describing themselves as 'natural' is a good thing, on the whole, and what is your opinion of the 'horse whisperers'?*

SYLVIA'S REPLY: I guess that 'natural' is a word that can be easily exploited, but I suppose, on the whole, it is good that people are exploring natural methods. The only thing I get worried about is 'the emperor's new clothes' syndrome. So often, people claim to have invented a new and natural method, and this is absolute nonsense. There are no new and natural methods. People have been working with horses since thousands of years before the birth of Christ, and I absolutely defy anyone to say that they have invented a new method. The biggest problem, to my mind, today is that people are not close enough to their horses, and if they try to emulate something artificially that is described as being special and natural (as though it were very revolutionary), they will be doomed to disappointment. Natural is what is natural to you and the horse – building up a relationship together, getting to know your horse, observing him, riding him, seeing what makes him happy, seeing what upsets him, appreciating when he does not understand, appreciating when he is not using himself correctly, and understanding what muscles should naturally be employed for everything that he does – that is natural. Just to say that something is natural by throwing away the rein or by sitting in a certain way is balderdash.

As for horse whisperers, again there is nothing new here. There have always been people with pretty amazing talents. I do not think that these things happen by magic. I think they come with experience and wisdom. I know myself, that my own particular talent for feeling, within my own mind, what the horse is feeling when a rider sits incorrectly or applies the wrong aid is something that has come probably through so much observation unconsciously done, that I now feel that it is a mental telepathy between me and the horse. I could say that this is a magical power that I have been given. I could also say that it is a gift from God. I am not sure – I think it is something that has come from years and years of experience. Perhaps in my desire to help the horse, it has been given to me a little more fully than it has to your average trainer. Horse whispering, I think, is a word that has been overused and is still inclined to be misused.

'these things do not happen by magic; they come with experience and wisdom'

I have met several horse whisperers in the past ten years, and I have to say that the only one who really impressed me was one who, like myself, has been with horses for several decades. I think his gift simply comes from observation and knowing what is right. I have met other horse whisperers who have talked nonsense, and in fact some of what has been described has been downright dangerous, in my opinion. I am very open minded; I would like to give everyone the benefit of the doubt, but I do have strong reservations about the public being taught these methods as though they were a magical cure for all. There is no magical cure with horses. There is far more to it than that, and anything that leads people into believing that it can all be learned from one consultation is, in my opinion, very sad and dishonest.

QUESTION 8: *What do you think of Monty Roberts' join-up technique?*

SYLVIA'S REPLY: I think the join-up technique is brilliant for horses who have a problem accepting human beings or accepting affection or discipline. I have watched Monty Roberts at work and have really been impressed, particularly with horses that have come straight in out of the herd, as it were, and have not been handled properly in the past.

I think that people who are close to their horses probably join-up the whole time, and to start by sending their horse away, having already been joined-up, can be a mistake. That is a side of the join-up technique that I do not like, as I do not ever like to teach a horse something and then reprimand him for having responded to it. If you have joined-up already, what on earth is the point of then telling the horse that he was wrong to have joined-up and that he has got to do it all over again? Imagine if we taught our children like that in kindergarten? As I said, I think that there is a lot of merit in it, but I think it has its use in a particular sphere – in other words handling young, difficult, or very green horses, also horses that have never really learned to trust. I am not altogether convinced of the need to join-up when there is a perfectly good trusting relationship already in existence.

QUESTION 9: *Why do you think that several 'modern' trainers seem to believe that lungeing is detrimental to horses?*

SYLVIA'S REPLY: I have to say that lungeing is something that I have always treated with respect and in moderation. I do remember at one time being given a difficult horse that I lunged for over a year twice daily with religious fervour and zeal. All I did with that horse was succeed in making him more and more fizzy, when in fact the opposite effect had been desired at the time. I thought that the more I lunged him, the more he would learn to quieten and settle down, but in his case it did not happen.

I think that lungeing has a great use as a preliminary to riding if the rider is worried that the horse could be too explosive. Therefore, from a safety point of view, they are trying to 'take the edge' off the horse's spirits. I also believe that lungeing is very useful at the beginning of training, or with the unbroken horse prior to placing the saddle on his back. This type of lungeing would be progressive. One would start with lungeing without a saddle, and gradually progress to lungeing with a saddle, and then hopefully progressing from there to the ridden work. What I do not like is seeing horses lunged for hours and hours. I think too much work on the circle can be detrimental.

With the best will in the world, the person on the end of the lunge cannot always dictate to the horse the frame in which he should be going. Side-reins definitely help, but a horse can learn to evade these quite well and still be very resistant to what is being asked of him. A horse, which should be ambidextrous, can still be just as stiff on one side despite having been lunged for hours on that side. He can compensate for what he is being asked to do by stiffening on the inner rein and shortening the outside of his body when he should be stretching.

I doubt whether lungeing is a cure for all. I think that it has its merits, and it would certainly be wrong to dismiss it out of hand. In my mind, the sooner I can get the horse off the lunge and into ridden work the happier I am.

However, I think it is wrong to tell people that it is not a good practice because it definitely does have its uses, and if it helps to avoid an accident with someone riding a very explosive horse, then it has to be good.

Summary and Conclusions

Sylvia Loch has spent a great many years studying the art of classical riding, and her achievements are great and numerous. She has incorporated her own sensitivity with the original gentle art of 'classicism'. She has also managed to bridge the gap for many everyday riders who hitherto believed classical riding to be beyond their ability. Her books and videos describe, in clear laymen's language, how to train the horse at almost every stage of training; showing the complete novice how to apply classical principles, even if they never intend to ride a dressage test. She has also shown how these principles are of benefit to every equestrian discipline, and her true empathy with the horse helps us all to look at training from the horse's point of view.

'Sylvia has managed to bridge the gap for riders who believed classical riding to be beyond their ability'

CHAPTER 3

Kelly Marks

A Gentle Give-and-Take Approach

'The idea of Intelligent Horsemanship is to take the best from both worlds – whether it is the Classical Riding Club or the farmer up the road'

K elly Marks is probably Monty Roberts' best known protégée in the UK. She is the originator of the Monty Roberts Educational Courses worldwide and the founder of 'Intelligent Horsemanship', an organization based in Oxfordshire, UK.

I have spoken to Kelly and read many of her magazine articles and her book *Perfect Manners* (Ebury Press 2002), as well as watching her work. Her approach to training seems to be kind, firm, and full of good, old-fashioned common sense. I found her appreciation that genetic alteration may have taken horses a long way from the 'zebra in our stable' very refreshing. This is an idea that seems to be logical, and a subject about which I have written articles in the past. Too many 'natural behaviourists' seem to ignore totally the fact that horses have evolved over many generations and have learned to adapt, very happily, to their lives with mankind. To always

'horses have evolved over generations and have learned to adapt to life with mankind'

assume that 'natural is best' can create an extremely cruel environment within which to keep a horse. Judging by Kelly's remarks in *Perfect Manners*, she understands well how nature can be cruel, while at the same time pointing out that we need to understand the nature of horses in the wild, in order to understand life from their viewpoint.

Foundation Exercises

In her book, Kelly describes her 'foundation exercises' which she advises are a first step in schooling using her methods. She starts with the coming-forward exercise, in which the aim is for the horse to come willingly right up to the handler from at least 10 feet away on a loose lead rope. Her advice is to stand away from the horse, initially at an angle of about 45 degrees. If your horse resists, you can increase the angle to about 90 degrees, and, using pressure from the rope, you can unbalance him, in order to initiate movement towards you. Kelly advocates that you are not in an aggressive stance and that you do not look the horse in the eye, but keep your eyes directed somewhere around his chest area.

Eye Contact

I found the issue of eye contact a particularly interesting point. Monty Roberts uses direct eye contact to move the horse away from him and avoids eye contact when he wants the horse to approach him. Kelly Marks is advocating the same principle, as I understand it, in other words that eye contact is perceived as aggressive from the horse's point of view. The Native American Indians use soft eye contact, coupled with focal concentration, to invite the horse to come towards them, in a very similar type of exercise, as described in Chapter 5 beginning on page 61. This, obviously, is a fundamental difference of opinion from Kelly's and Monty's shared view.

Kelly goes on to describe how to ask the horse to back up, giving a series of short pushes on the rope, rewarding him as soon as he takes the smallest step backwards. Kelly maintains that if you step away from your horse with eyes lowered and arms together; he should step towards you. If you want him to stay where he is as you walk backwards, then you give him eye contact and keep your arms wide open.

I think that whether or not the horse does in fact perceive eye contact as being aggressive will make little difference to his ability to learn this exercise. When he receives positive reinforcement for performing the required movement, he will soon learn to associate the body language from the handler, whichever way it is presented to him. Horses are quite clever!

Give-and-Take Approach

Kelly goes on to describe how to teach your horse to step sideways, in a way that I would consider to be fairly conventional. She uses pressure with the hand on the horse's side, about where a rider's heel would be, coupled with a verbal request of 'over'. She goes on to describe some more advanced backing-up exercises using poles placed on the ground in an 'L' shape. Some of these exercises may sound similar to other 'natural horsemanship' techniques. However, I found that the way in which Kelly advises us to put these into practice to be different. She has a very gentle give-and-take approach, and gives the impression that nothing should be approached too abruptly. In addition, throughout *Perfect Manners*, Kelly makes repeated reference to the need for us to bear in mind the possibility of physical unsoundness in the horse, as a reason for resistance, and the need, maybe, to call in professional help, be it veterinary or complementary therapy.

'the possibility of physical unsoundness in the horse as a reason for resistance'

Kelly, along with other trainers, advocates the use of gently touching the horse all over and only approaching the ticklish spots gradually, when the horse is relaxed about the procedure.

Kelly goes on to describe further yielding exercises, such as head-lowering, neck-flexing, and exercises involving moving away from the pressure of a rope. These exercises are all done gradually and gently with the horse remaining stress-free. She describes an exercise called 'disengaging the hindquarters'. This is similar to the turn on the forehand, except that the front legs are allowed to move forward in a small circle. This could be a useful exercise to teach from the ground and one which, if carried out tactfully, should not put the horse under any strain.

She also describes how to move the forehand around the hindquarters, in a similar way to a pirouette. However, she prefers backward movement to any forward movement, the idea being that forward movement will drop weight onto the forehand instead of taking it back onto the hindquarters. This is contrary to the instruction of the classical masters, in that they advocate a forward rhythm being upheld. In order to keep the rhythm of the walk, the horse is obliged to bring his inside hind leg further underneath him, thereby flexing and strengthening the joints. In this way, his hindquarters are built up to give him the strength to be able to take more weight on his hindquarters. Nevertheless, Kelly's application of this movement is a useful exercise to teach your horse from the ground.

She also describes how to teach your horse to walk from left to right directly in front of you and also to walk straight in front of you. These exercises have a multitude of practical uses in everyday life, such as when leading your horse through a gateway on a windy day. You can stand still holding the gate while the horse walks through.

Join-Up

As would be expected, Kelly uses join-up in the same way as Monty Roberts. However, she seems to be advocating that we establish a trusting bond with our horse before we start join-up. Although this may seem, on the surface, a different approach from Monty's, perhaps we should take into account the context in which Monty usually operates. We normally see him giving displays of join-up in demonstration evenings, with an audience, where he has only a limited amount of time to spend with each horse. In addition, the vast majority of people watching would probably disbelieve and belittle his techniques if that were not the first time that he had seen the horse. Kelly is giving advice to her readers and students on how the owners should start with their own horses, which is slightly different.

'horses are not designed to work repetitively in small circles...'

Kelly describes an alternative to join-up, where the horse is attached to a long line. In other ways, it is the same as join-up, in that the handler stands at 45 degrees behind the horse (not in the usual lungeing position), using the same body language as described by Monty Roberts and summarized in Chapter 7 beginning on page 89. This method may not be quite so clear to the horse as being loose during join-up, but may be useful if an enclosed area is not available.

Kelly also recognises instances when join-up would not be appropriate for varying reasons to do with the horse and also the handler. Some examples are as follows:

- A very young horse who is nervous and an inexperienced handler.
- An aggressive horse and an inexperienced handler.
- Bottle-reared or over-handled foals, when there is more value in working on her foundation exercises as briefly outlined in the beginning of this chapter and more fully described in Kelly's book *Perfect Manners*.

Lungeing

Kelly, like Monty, is against conventional lungeing. She maintains that a heavy cavesson with the line attached to the horse's nose puts an unnatural weight on the front of the horse's nose, and that the horse has to tip his head to the outside to counterbalance that weight. She also says that horses are not designed to work repetitively in small circles, and that this can damage joints, ligaments and tendons. She sites a study done by Texas A & M University, where X-rays were taken of horses' legs before and after six weeks of 'light' lungeing. The results apparently showed considerable unnatural calcification of the joints.

Kelly, however, advocates lungeing with two lines as in long-reining, keeping the horse in better balance, and creating bilateral pressure. In addition, there is more scope for variation in the work, as you can go off on a straight line, or round the fields when desired.

My opinion differs from Kelly's on the above points for the following reasons.

First, the weight of a lunge cavesson is really not that great, particularly taking into account the weight of a horse's head.

Second, I have seen horses turning their heads to the outside while at liberty, both during join-up and during loose-schooling. In the dressage world, this is called counter-flexion. It is a natural thing for the horse to do when unbalanced,

'it causes horses to 'switch off' to body language'

for whatever reason for example, age, lack of training and/or fitness etc. I quote here from Paul Belasik's book *Dressage for the 21st Century* (JA Allen 2002): 'Bending to the outside forces the horse out of balance and to lean like a bicycle on the turn.' Horses can be unbalanced on the lunge, as well as at any other time, and they usually are unbalanced when their education on the lunge begins. One of the main reasons for lungeing is to help the horse to achieve flexibility, strength, and the all-important balance, so that the well-trained horse will turn his head to the inside during turns and circles. I quote again from the book mentioned above: 'The principle of inside bend remains unshakeable because of its simple but important physics: it remains one of the cornerstones of classical dressage. Almost all of the classical lateral exercises a rider/trainer uses in practise are aimed at perfecting this ability, and this work begins unmounted on the lunge line.'

Third, six weeks of lungeing, presumably every day, is an extreme amount. Although the sessions may have been considered 'light', even light lungeing is recognised by good trainers as being hard work, particularly for young or unfit horses. This is why, in good classical training, everything is done gently and for short periods at a time with a slow build up, and lungeing would not be carried out every day, especially not with an unfit horse. In fact, it is my guess that six weeks of any kind of daily work with a young or unfit horse could produce unnatural calcification of the joints, if sufficient time were not given for the horse to build up his strength.

Basically, the smaller the circle, the harder work it is for the horse to perform, whether on the lunge or under saddle. In addition, the larger the horse, the more strenuous it will be for him to execute small circles. However, the purpose of good training is to gradually build up his strength, over a period of years (not weeks, or even months) so that he can perform circle work without strain. How else would a horse ever be strong enough to execute say, a canter pirouette, if the trainer did not meticulously build up the horse's strength slowly in smaller and smaller canter circles, over a long period of time beforehand?

Fourth, the point made that long-reining keeps the horse in better balance does, in my opinion, have some validity. Is this not why we normally use side-reins? As long as the side-reins are of an appropriate length, they will serve exactly the same purpose as the long-lines. It is important, however, that they should not be too short for the stage of training of the horse, and that the horse's head is not pulled towards his chest. A young or unschooled horse would require a much longer side-rein than a more advanced horse.

There are further reasons why Kelly is against lungeing (see her comments on pages 38–39), such as that she says it causes horses to 'switch off' to body language. She maintains that this does not normally happen with long-reining, as the horse seems to know 'this is exercise mode now' instead of 'this is communication time'. I personally cannot see the difference, from the psychological point of view, between long-reining and lungeing.

Kelly also dislikes the fact that during lungeing we are putting pressure on one side of the horse, expecting him to go forward. She believes that this will confuse him when we ask for sideways movements in the saddle, as pressure from one side will then mean move sideways. I have never found this to be a problem for any horse, as the whip should be used as a guide and extension to the handler's body. When the whip is held slightly behind the quarters, this means go forward. When it is held towards the girth area, it means go outwards, or in other words, sideways. This is one way of varying the work on the lunge for a horse who is sufficiently fit. He can be asked to move outwards and gently spiral inwards on the circle. Provided he is sufficiently prepared for this relatively strenuous exercise, it is a very good movement to increase strength and suppleness, adding interest to the work. I have always found that lungeing consolidates the work under saddle and in no way contradicts it.

'turning the head to the outside is a natural thing for the horse to do when unbalanced'

QUESTION 1: *I know that you have said in your book that it is not advisable to use join-up on all horses, for various reasons – many of which are to do with the handler not having enough experience. But have you ever come across a remedial horse that did not respond to join-up? If this were the case, would you then revert to your foundation exercises?*

KELLY'S REPLY: If you find that a horse is not responding to join-up – and it may be because of you, the handler, or it may be some issues with the horse – I say do not go on longer than five minutes. Just halt the process, give him a stroke and go back to handling – halter-work exercises. When you work with a horse who has problems, the first thing you want to do is to create a bond of trust and respect. There are three ways to do this. The oldest way to create this bond is time – you groom the horse, lead him around, love him and stroke him, and in six months if you are lucky, or maybe 18 months, you have a trust with the horse. Those of us being sent horses with problems often do not have that time, so we have to work that much more quickly, and the ideas that we use are based on behaviour.

The only way a horse can show leadership in the wild is to move another horse around. One really good way to do that is with halter work, and you just keep moving the horse around. The other way of course is join-up. It can be great; as long as you always know that you are using it to create a bond of trust and respect with the horse, you will never go wrong. You will never say 'the horse would not drop his head, so I sent him around for two hours' or 'the horse would not go away, so I gave him a good beating', because you would have lost the whole point of why you are doing it. Therefore, my idea is that you must do what feels right for you as well. For instance, I would not do join-up on a very tiny pony, because to do join-up well I would need to be two foot high. We must all make judgements as best we can at the time.

QUESTION 2: *Do you think that horses who have done join-up on more than one occasion would become confused if later asked to lunge or to be driven? I ask this as join-up obviously concentrates on body language, and while being driven a horse has to listen carefully to verbal commands.*

KELLY'S REPLY: I think that some horses get confused when they are lunged anyway, because of inconsistent body language from the person lungeing. If they look the horse in the eye one minute and then drop their shoulders and look down because they are not thinking about their body language, you then see horses start to come in and then the handler uses the whip. This is when the horse gets switched off. I believe in a system of lungeing that works with body language. It is on a longer line; the person in the middle uses consistent body language and walks in a kind of oval, so that they can keep themselves slightly behind the horse to drive on. I think that this can work very well.

When you talk of horses to be driven – if you mean long-reining – horses adapt very well to long-reining after join-up because they realise that it is something different. Furthermore, with long-reining you tend to keep just behind the horse – again in the driving position – rather than what I feel is the unnatural 'at the shoulder' position. I feel that this position has the effect of pushing the horse out from the shoulder. We always try to stay just behind, so we are pushing the horse on.

'the oldest way to create a bond of trust and respect is time…'

If you mean horses driven in carts – we have had lots of horses go on to work well between shafts after join-up, and they will learn verbal commands when they are being long-reined, so there is not a problem with that at all.

QUESTION 3: *Do you think that everyone should do join-up with their horse, regardless of whether they already feel closely bonded?*

KELLY'S REPLY: No, I feel that join-up should remain optional for all people. If you think it will benefit the horse and yourself, then that is great. I have seen a lot of horse/human relationships really benefit from doing join-up. People come on courses with their horses, and join-up has really made some vast improvements. However, nobody should feel that it is something that they have to do, and of course if they were going to do it badly, it would not be very helpful.

QUESTION 4: *Do you know whether the cruel 'breaking-in' practices, for example sacking out and so on, as described by Monty Roberts in his book, are still commonplace in the world today? Or do you think that the world is now becoming, in general, more enlightened?*

KELLY'S REPLY: I live, as most of us do, in my own closed little world with lovely students and people who are really interested in making things nicer for horses, so I had started thinking the same way that maybe you are. Then, on my recent tour of 21 dates in the UK, I have met three horses who have had a leg tied up and gone through the 'sacking out' process, hit with plastic bags or whatever. An Argentinian gentleman has set up in Yorkshire, most disturbingly describing himself as a 'horse whisperer'. He has brought Argentinian methods to Yorkshire, and he is working with horses and is now taking them in as a professional. I have met someone who took a horse to his yard, with no idea of what was going to go on. Three or four weeks later, the horse was in a terrible state when she came to get him back. There is also someone in Wiltshire who is doing the same thing.

We met another horse in Scotland who had been due to be put down the week before, but they saved him for us. Grant* rode him successfully, and we are going to continue with him. We met a little three-year old Exmoor gelding in Reading, and apparently there is a lady in Reading describing herself as a 'horse whisperer', who tied the pony's back foot to his headcollar, to 'teach him a lesson', when the pony was two years old. This obviously terrified the life out of him. His owner is very nice and is trying to build the pony's confidence in people again. So, it is very sad that this type of cruel practice almost seems to be coming back in some ways.

' she tied the pony's back foot to his headcollar, to teach him a lesson'

(*Grant Bazin has a similar equestrian background to Kelly. He was a junior show jumper and then went into racing, but always felt that he would like to treat horses in a gentler way. He is completely in agreement with Kelly's methods, and they often work together during demonstrations.)*

QUESTION 5: *What do you think of the competition scene today (including dressage, eventing and show jumping) in terms of the welfare of the horse?*

KELLY'S REPLY: I do not have enough to do with any of those three disciplines full-time to give a properly considered view on it. Having read Nick Skelton's autobiography, I felt very pleased to be out of show jumping. It seems a very hard life for all concerned.

Eventing – marvellous what they do, but I wouldn't want my horse, Pie, jumping those solid fences. I am very pleased to see that they now use some sort of catch, so that the fences will collapse, otherwise obviously the horses are going to break their legs and necks, and that is not nice!

Occasionally we get remedial dressage horses come to us, and the problem they have had with their owners is usually that they are nappy or will not go forward. Usually this is because they have been over-collected for too long. The owners say that he suddenly bolts for no reason at all. These horses have been asked to be in a collected position for so long and not allowed to relax, that they have to burst away as it were. I went to see the Anky Van Grunsen demonstration at Addington earlier this year, and I was very impressed. She was constantly emphasizing how you need to let your horses stretch and relax. I am quite sure that these things don't happen to her, but again it is people who do not have sympathy for the horse, that these things happen to.

QUESTION 6: *I know that you are a member of the Classical Riding Club. Do you find that there are similarities in your training techniques and the classical approach to training?*

KELLY'S REPLY: I bet there are hundreds. Two that come to mind are rewarding the horse and sympathy with the horse. One of the reasons I joined CRC is the fact that I like Sylvia Loch's writing. She obviously loves horses and is very sympathetic to them; that is very important.

QUESTION 7: *Do you think that we are in danger of becoming 'alternative training and therapy' mad, in other words that we may become close-minded to some of the sound traditional methods? Is it possible to take the best out of both worlds?*

KELLY'S REPLY: Certainly it is. The idea of Intelligent Horsemanship is to take the best from both worlds – whether it is the Classical Riding Club or the farmer up the road. If they have methods that work for horses, then we can integrate them into our system.

Intelligent Horsemanship was looked upon as 'alternative training', but nowadays we are becoming frighteningly mainstream. If you ring the British Horse Society saying you have a problem with a horse, they are very likely to put you on to us. We now have vets coming on our courses. At veterinary colleges they have all this fantastic scientific education, but at no stage are they told how to approach a horse. We also work for the RSPCA and Redwings Horse Sanctuary. I have a wonderful letter from Joy Pritchard of the Brooke Hospital for Animals. She is their main vet going all over the world. She came on a five-day course and thought it was fantastic, and she has given a full report on it.

We have also started work for the British Jockey Club, helping racehorses to go into the starting stalls better. A lot of racehorses are still having electric shock treatment used on them. There was even one trainer who put his horse on the horse walker for 12 hours every day, with no food or water. After three days he put food and water in the starting stalls to get him to go in – it is just horrific. You have to gain a horse's confidence to go in – not make him go in like that.

People may consider that we are a bit 'soft', because we do not like using whips and we look at things from the horse's point of view, instead of saying 'it just needs teaching a lesson'. However, if we were not effective, we would not have a job and in this way Intelligent Horsemanship, as an organization, has survived the test of time. We have been operating Intelligent Horsemanship for eight years now, and it is actually growing in strength. We have a sympathetic approach, but we have to be effective as well. 'Alternative' methods have to prove themselves to work; they are no good if they are just a lot of talk.

One of the things about the old-fashioned training that we prefer to steer clear of is the habit of shouting, screaming and humiliating pupils, which I cannot stand. I was taught in a way that was not very nice, and I would never want to do that to my students. I have come around now to thinking that if a student does not understand, it is my responsibility to get the student to understand – the same as it is with the horse. What we teachers have got to do is to find better ways of explaining things, and that is what we are working on all the time. One of the things that people comment upon when they come on our courses is the friendly atmosphere – and they seem surprised at this. Yes, of course, we want people to have a good time.

There are many sound traditional methods that we use. One instance that I talk about in demonstrations is that in the old days we were always told that you should lead your horse the last half mile home. People just do not seem to do that nowadays, and they practise that worst piece of horsemanship of riding the horse right back to the stable. Apart from not allowing the horse to cool down and settle, you have horses who want to get to the stable all the time instead of learning to relax on a ride, because they are not always quite sure when the rider is going to get off.

QUESTION 8: *Apart from the obviously huge influence of Monty Roberts, are there any other trainers or methods that you have come across over the years which still influence you?*

KELLY'S REPLY: Not specifically. It is all the experiences put together that influence me. I am an avid reader. I think that Linda Tellington-Jones' books are excellent. I think that she does a lot of good work, and I am a big fan of hers, as I am of Mary Bromiley, who funnily enough is a big fan of Linda Tellington-Jones and Monty Roberts. I think that Mary Wanless is great, as well as Sylvia Loch.

I have just seen a book by Perry Wood called *Real Riding* – I think that is really interesting. He has a nice attitude. I have always been a big 'fan', ever since the days of Marion Coakes and Stroller of showjumping fame.

Summary and Conclusions

Although I have pointed out a number of differences between our approaches, I still feel that Kelly is very much 'on the side of the horse' and does not adopt a rigid methodology. Her book is full of sound advice, and she gives alternatives. For instance, if you still want to lunge, she gives tips on how to minimize any possible damaging effects, all of which is good advice. Throughout her book *Perfect Manners*, she is liberal with safety hints, for both horse and handler, which no one should ignore.

I found Kelly's attitude towards join-up and the lungeing debate to be somewhat more flexible than Monty Roberts'. This is probably because of their different equestrian backgrounds. As I have said before, I think Monty's attitude has been engendered through a very severe upbringing and is very understandable. He is unflinching in his defence of the horse, whereas I would hope that Kelly has not seen the same degree of brutality in the UK, and can therefore be slightly more flexible in her approach.

Although I differ with Kelly on several points, I heartily agree with her ideals on the whole. I believe that we are lucky to have such an empathetic trainer in this country.

Having talked with Kelly at some length, I know that she is very interested in classical riding and has joined the Classical Riding Club. However, the time available for her to investigate this ancient art is extremely limited, owing to her very important role as a remedial trainer. Many of the remedial horses that she has to deal with would be most horsemen's nightmare! It is very sad to report that there are horses in the UK today who have been so badly abused that they are quite wild and dangerous. Some inhuman people still use electric prods on horses! Little wonder they are terrified and wild. I would not wish to take on the task of curing these poor creatures of their fears and phobias. I am only thankful that there are trainers like Kelly Marks and others who are able and willing to do so.

'*alternative methods have to prove themselves to work;
they are no good if they are just a lot of talk*'

CHAPTER 4

Richard Maxwell

A Commonsense Approach

*'If you cannot find a conventional or an
unconventional process that horses can
understand, you have to start to modify it'*

Richard Maxwell has achieved success as a trainer in dealing with a large number of problem equines, has written several books, and appeared on the UK television programme *Pet Rescue* on numerous occasions. During these programmes, he has demonstrated the ability to communicate in a kind, quiet and caring manner, with horses and ponies who have been severely traumatized, before being rescued by such organizations as the International League for the Protection of Horses. His gentle, non-confrontational way of dealing with these animals was most impressive. Equally as impressive was the success with which he changed the horse's behaviour and attitude towards humans. I was pleased that he did not expect a hitherto terrified horse to suddenly become calm and obedient, but after only about ten minutes, the animal was showing definite signs of responding and gaining in confidence.

'it would be like saying to a dyslexic – you have to learn to read this way'

Although he is one of the few people in the UK who is authorized to practise Monty Roberts' techniques during these programmes he did not use the join-up technique, presumably because the horses were too traumatized by their previous encounters with mankind. The main technique that I observed was one of advance and retreat, using plenty of passive body language and a soothing voice.

The Beginnings

Richard Maxwell's contact with horses started when he was only about three years old. His mother was involved with horses, and he was the typical child who always wanted a pony but could not have one, and had to wait until later in life before he could own a horse. He was not very happy at school, but it was not until the age of 28 that he found out that he was, in fact, dyslexic. This has been an important factor in his attitude towards problem horses, which he sees as having 'learning difficulties'. Max (as Richard is more commonly known) explained to me:

'If you cannot find a conventional or an unconventional process that these horses can understand, you then have to start to modify it. You cannot say – you have to learn in this way, which would be like saying to a dyslexic – you have to learn to read this way. There are various forms of dyslexia and various ways of dealing with it. This is what has provoked a lot of my thinking in the training of horses.'

From the age of 12, it was horses non-stop for Max. Later, he joined the army, went to the Household Cavalry where he became a riding instructor, and met Monty Roberts two years before leaving the army. This two-year period, I presume, must have been fairly conflicting for Max, since he was deeply involved in conventional equine training and, at the same time, being educated in unconventional techniques. However, it did teach him that sound principles run right across the board in horsemanship wherever they occur, be it in the military, classical or alternative techniques. Max very well understands that classical principles have been tested, re-tested and confirmed through centuries of riding and training and to turn your back on that because we now have alternative ways of doing things would be the greatest folly.

His Philosophy

Max has therefore learned to become a 'sponge' for equine knowledge and to take the best of any new techniques, from wherever they come, as well as keeping the best from his previous knowledge and never discarding anything out of hand. In this way, he aims to do the best he possibly can for his own enrichment, as well as that of his own horses and any with which he comes into contact.

As would be expected, much of Max's philosophy is similar to that of Kelly Marks. However, they are different people and have their own individual interpretations to certain aspects of training. This, in my opinion, is a healthy state of affairs. I would be rather worried if they trained in exactly the same way in every detail. The inference would then be that they were behaving as automatons and merely doing what they were told. Happily, this is not the case; a certain amount of leeway for personal interpretation appears to be allowed.

'most ridden horses today are only distantly related to wild creatures…'

Max does not adhere to the unswerving *au naturel* method sometimes adopted nowadays. He understands that the needs of horses differ greatly. He also realises that most ridden horses today are only distantly related to wild creatures, having been domesticated for many hundreds of years. However, he does remind us that they are inherently claustrophobic, I quote from one of his books *Understanding Your Horse* (David & Charles 1996): 'It is essential to understand that horses are claustrophobic, for this affects their attitude to stabling and being transported in lorries and trailers.' The fact that they are willing and relaxed about standing in a stable or being transported in a lorry demonstrates how keen they are to please us when they have confidence in their handler/rider.

I believe (as Max does) that, when conditions allow, we should turn our horses out to grass each day to play and relax. However, there are circumstances where this is not in the horse's best interests (Max and I are in full agreement here). This is a subject on which I feel strongly, and Richard Maxwell is not the only trainer to describe the horse as claustrophobic. I will therefore delve deeper into this subject in Chapter 12, General Issues and Conclusions, at the end of this book.

I am pleased to see that Max advocates the use of vocal communication from the trainer. Having heard and seen him in action, I certainly found his voice soothing. He also recommends plenty of physical communication, in the form of rewards with stroking and gentle patting.

In *Understanding Your Horse*, Max describes in detail the differing body language of horses at various ages and in different situations, as well as their vocal communications. He makes the point that there is a difference between passive and submissive body language. The latter is not what we want to convey to the horse.

Along with most trainers, Richard Maxwell advocates that we should create a partnership with our horse, but we should always be the leader. He stresses that horses expect and require our leadership. He advocates that there should be a 51 per cent balance in favour of the human, and this sounds perfectly sensible to me.

To be a good leader for our horse, Max tells us that we must try to behave more like an equine leader would, in say a herd situation, rather than like a predator. If we can instil this kind of confidence in our horse, then he will be content to stand in a stable and be transported in a lorry, because he has put his trust in us. However, we do not create this confidence by an aggressive domination; Max's methods are much more subtle. (Further details about my own interpretation and beliefs of a good horse/human relationship are presented in Chapter 12, General Issues and Conclusions.)

'a well-handled four-year-old is less likely to rebel when he starts work…'

Max points out that horses have learned to understand a few of our words, but that we have not bothered to learn much of their language – fair comment! They communicate via their body language all the time. Their language is universal; a horse from this country could communicate with any other horse from a different continent. My only point of contention here is that I believe that most horses, and certainly those who spend a considerable amount of time with their humans, actually understand much more than just a few of our words! I do agree, however, that many of us pay scant attention to their language.

Youngsters

In his book, Max also describes the handling, leading and various first lessons from day one of the foal's arrival. He poses the question of whether it is best to 'turn the horse away' after the initial handling period, usually when he becomes a yearling. The practice of 'turning away' has been utilized for many years and is, from a physical point of view, excellent for the growth and development of the youngster. Max makes the valid point that the foal still has to have his feet trimmed, be wormed and have inoculations. It seems rather unfair to bring him out of the field only for these treatments, which may not be perceived by the horse as particularly pleasant. In addition, allowing him to live in a field for the first three or four years of his life, doing just as he pleases, may not be the best way to prepare him for his future life. If he is brought in at, say, four years old and is then suddenly expected to start work on a daily basis, he is much more likely to rebel than if he had been having regular interaction with humans in the intervening period.

I agree with this point of view. When my own mare was a yearling, I did not turn her away. I certainly did not ask her to do any physical work, but I did teach her the vocal commands of 'walk on', 'halt' and so on, as well as walking her in hand on the road and around the farm. This was perhaps only once or twice per week, but she was handled every day, learning to wear boots and rugs, and experiencing all sorts of human-related things, such as plastic bags. When it became time for me to start backing her, it seemed like a natural progression; she thoroughly enjoyed the process. She appeared to not even notice when a saddle was placed on her back. After months of leaning over her back, when I finally mounted her, the only reaction she showed was one of pleasure and 'do I get another carrot now?'

The only thing against this approach to youngsters is, as I mentioned previously, that many people do not know when to stop. If they do not turn their yearlings away, they may be tempted to over-lunge them or even to ride them, and this could obviously be disastrous. If there is the slightest danger of this happening, then it is probably preferable for them to be 'turned away'. Common sense and discretion should be used in all things.

Lungeing

Max appears to be far less anti-lungeing than Monty Roberts is. He still prefers lungeing with two reins (long-reining on a circle) for some of the same reasons that Monty is against lungeing with a single rein. Max's main objection is the weight of the lunge caves-son, which is believed to cause the horse to turn his head to the outside of the circle (see Chapter 12, General Issues and Conclusions, for further discussion on this point).

'lungeing is an important part of a young horse's education…'

Nevertheless, he does recognise lungeing as an important part of a young horse's education. He advocates the start of this work when the horse is between two and three years old. He says that the duration of this work, which should be kept to just walk and trot, can be built up to a maximum of ten minutes at a time. I definitely agree with this. So many people do not seem to know when to stop! Five or ten minutes twice a week is very much preferable to 30 minutes once per week. In fact, 30 minutes is a long time for any horse to work on the lunge, however fit and at whatever age.

Max's way of long-reining appears to be similar to the classical Dutch style, in other words the outside rein being brought behind the horse's quarters. He describes how working on transitions and stops in this way helps the horse to learn balance and insti-gates the use of the hindquarters, making it easier when the time comes for him to carry the weight of a rider. This is in line with sound classical principles.

Join-Up

Max uses join-up in a similar way to Monty Roberts, except that for the past three years he has not used a round pen. Instead, he normally starts with halter work and the actual join-up, if used, is done on a 20 foot (17m) rope. This is described in more detail in Question 3 of the interview with Max.

He makes the point quite strongly in his books (as does Kelly Marks), that the first thing he looks at, when faced with a problem horse, is whether the animal is in physical pain. This is an extremely common occurrence. For instance, horses that rear often have pain in the neck or mouth; horses that buck often have back pain; and horses that pull are often running away from pain in the mouth (a possible teeth problem). This is a very important point, and one that can be overlooked, particularly by inexperienced owners. Sometimes, long after the pain has been alleviated, the memory of the pain will still be there, causing the horse to behave in the same manner, in anticipation of the pain he expects. Horses often develop a habit of moving in a certain way to protect themselves from discomfort or pain, even after the pain has been reduced or removed.

'the memory of pain can sometimes cause the horse to behave in the same manner…'

This appears to be where Max uses the join-up technique most frequently. Join-up in this situation creates the beginning of a trusting partnership, following which Max can continue to work the horse from the ground. Long-reining from the ground can then retrain the way the horse moves. If the horse is schooled at liberty, say on the circle, he is most likely to continue to move in the habitual way.

The join-up technique is described in detail in Chapter 7 on Monty Roberts, and Max's adaptations are described later in his interview (Question 3).

Backing

Max's approach to backing is gradual. He mouths the horse for a few days before backing, so that wearing the bridle is no problem. His approach differs from Monty Roberts' methods, which I have seen, in that he lies across the horse's back before putting on the saddle. His reasoning for this is that he has already established a good relationship with the horse, and it is just an extension of this trust for the horse to allow him to lean over his back. The horse is not restrained, and Max does not have a leg-up from a third party. The horse will often turn around and be curious about what is happening, but he very rarely moves away. This good relationship prior to backing is probably a luxury that Monty Roberts does not usually have, as his methods are constantly being challenged, and he has a need to prove them on previously untouched animals, often with limited time.

After Max is satisfied that the horse has felt his weight on either side of his back and the saddle is subsequently put on, the horse is then long-reined. He is taught to turn in each direction and eventually to rein-back. Only then does Max start the mounting procedure. I personally feel that the rein-back, if executed correctly, is quite a difficult and advanced movement, and therefore do not think it appropriate at this early stage. However, Max feels that if it is not taught at this stage, the horse may use reverse gear as an evasion against the handler/rider.

Before he mounts, Max puts weight in the stirrup as well as leaning over his back. He does this from both sides. Again, he does this unaided. I appreciate his motives for this, but I feel that a helper to hold the opposite stirrup would be better for the horse, so that the saddle is not pulled across the horse's back. With some horses, because of their conformation, it is virtually impossible for the saddle not to move when weight goes into one stirrup. The temptation in this circumstance is to do the girth up very tightly. This can obviously be extremely uncomfortable, not to mention unnerving, for the young horse.

Once he is mounted, Max will walk and trot the horse around the arena or enclosure on both reins. This will be repeated over the following few days, before the horse is ready to be taken outside the enclosed area where backing has taken place.

Handling and Leading

Max's advice on this subject is not dissimilar to that of Kelly Marks. He points out how dangerous it can be when the handler uses what he terms 'traditional' leading methods. He says: 'A potential hazard with the conventional method of leading is that, as the handler is so close to the horse's front, he is in a vulnerable position if it suddenly leaps forwards.' I think that this comment is valid in many cases, and his advice as given in detail in *Understanding Your Horse* seems very sensible. I am pleased that he also stresses the need for tact when using halters or devices that apply poll pressure. The horse's poll is a sensitive area, and the use of these devices by inexperienced handlers has worried me for some time. However, I recognise that they have their uses, and are invaluable in certain circumstances. The safety of both people and horses must be of paramount importance. It is foolhardy (and unfair to the animal) to lead a horse in an ordinary headcollar in a public place, unless the handler is 100 per cent sure of his ability to stay in control.

'traditional leading methods put the handler in a vulnerable position'

Difficult-to-Catch Horses

On this subject, Max seems to have an almost unique solution – although it is always possible that some everyday horse owners have used this technique before. Since horses have been domesticated for so long, it would be almost impossible to have a technique that is totally unique. Nevertheless, good ideas can be born independently, and this is one that would seem well worth a try if all else fails, as long as you can set aside a whole day for the process and, of course, have plenty of patience.

Most modern trainers seem to advise the use of passive body language, as well as the advance-and-retreat system (see Chapter 7 on Monty Roberts). However, Max has encountered a horse that did not respond to any of the usual tactics. His advice in this case is to 'walk the horse down'. You should go into the field and attempt to catch the horse as usual. When the horse moves away, you walk after him, do not chase him, just walk, but keep walking and do not allow the horse to rest and graze.

Most horses will soon become bored with this process and, being unable to settle to graze, they will turn to the handler and offer themselves to be caught. However, the confirmed 'bad catcher' has been known to carry on with this game for hours, so be prepared and be patient. However, after this initial time, subsequent attempts should take progressively less time before the horse gives in. Eventually, you should end up with a horse that is a joy to bring in from the field!

I have a hint, which I have used with some success with horses who may be slightly head shy, or maybe they are just teasing! Most horse people will know the scenario: the horse allows you to approach and caress him, then just as you are about to slip the headcollar over his nose, off he goes. The obvious thing to do here is to turn the horse out wearing his headcollar (bearing in mind the safety aspect – making sure that the headcollar will break should it become caught up in a hedge or fence). However, this does not always solve the problem of the head-shy horse who does not like the feel of the headcollar as it goes over his ears. My tip here is to catch the horse in the normal way with the headcollar that is on the horse, and then to gently fit another headcollar over the top. In this way, the horse learns that the operation of fitting the headcollar is not unpleasant, and at the same time he has already been caught. Obviously, the aim is eventually to be able to turn the horse out without the need for him to wear a headcollar at all.

'a tap with the whip, when the leg is ignored, is far kinder than continual nagging with the legs'

Ridden Work

Richard Maxwell appears to have a good understanding of many classical principles, including the need for the horse to respond to a light touch of the rider's leg. He understands that a tap with the whip, when the leg is ignored, is far kinder than continual nagging with the legs. He also has a good understanding of the way in which the well-schooled horse can take more weight on the hind legs, thus lifting the forehand, making for a lighter, more harmonious ride.

Napping, Running Backwards and Rearing

Max addresses these problems with tact and continually refers to the need to check for a physical reason for the problem, such as a painful back, badly fitting tack, teeth problems and so on. He advocates the use of the 'soft rope', which looks similar to Monty's 'Wip Wop Rope', for several problems. One such problem is to attract the attention of a horse that is prone to shying (in the case of a horse who seems to be just looking for something to shy at, as opposed to a horse who is genuinely frightened). For the horse who runs backwards (presuming that the use of a strong leg aid to move forwards has failed), Max's advice is to try to turn the horse in either direction or, if feasible, allowing him to back into a prickly hedge or something solid.

Max tells me that after meeting a very gifted man called Andy Andrews, he came to realise that 95 per cent of all behavioural problems in horses were caused by physiological pain. Although he had always looked into the possibility of back pain and so on, he had never quite realised how necessary it is to acquire second or even third opinions, as it is so easy for vets or other professionals to miss the source of many types of pain. The late Andy Andrews was a self-taught chiropractor/osteopath, and was obviously a clever and sensitive person. Max reports that his own success rate with unrideable horses used to be around 40 per cent. After working with Andy, Max's success rate suddenly shot up to 85–90 per cent. There will always be a few horses who have genuinely had the source of their pain removed, but who still buck or rear as a conditioned or habitual response.

The fact that Andy Andrews has now passed away is a source of great regret, not only to Max but also to any caring horse person. However, we must be duly grateful for the knowledge that he has passed on to Richard Maxwell. The above figures are certainly food for thought, and I doubt if there are many horsemen who, if they are honest, are not cringing and feeling extremely guilty for the unintentional pain they may have inflicted on difficult horses in the past. I count myself among these people, as does Max.

Bucking

Bucking can fall into two different categories. There are those *joie de vivre* bucks, which the excited, over-fresh horse, cannot seem to help himself from performing out of sheer joy. However, I concur with Max here, in that he ought to be taught not to do this when under saddle, as it may become a habit. If he needs to buck to let off steam, then Max advises that he should be given plenty of time at liberty in the field. Personally, I find that loose schooling is a much better way of ensuring that the horse has a good 'playtime'. I have enlarged upon this in Chapter 12, General Issues and Conclusions. Every horse should be taught that bucking is not the thing to do while carrying a rider. That is not to say, however, that we cannot allow the young horse (or any horse perhaps) the occasional indiscretion, without being too hard on him, depending upon the circumstances.

'the most common reason for serious bucking is back pain…'

The other category of bucking is really designed to dislodge the rider. The most common reason for this is back pain, but can be pain in the shoulder, neck, or badly fitting tack. I once knew a horse who was a confirmed bucker. Her bucks were so horrendous, reminiscent of a handstand, that very few people could stay on. All the usual sources of pain and discomfort had been ruled out, until one day a different vet attended the yard and diagnosed a serious stifle problem. She had a successful operation on her stifle, and I do not think that she ever bucked again. Everyone who had ever ridden her, including myself, felt very guilty for having put her through what must have been excruciating pain.

Max used to use a device he called 'the gumline'. This is similar to the 'buck-stopper' used by Monty Roberts. It consists of a piece of soft rope that slips under the top lip. If the horse does not buck, then this is not intended to cause any discomfort. It comes into play if the horse puts his head down to buck. Basically, the horse is inflicting pain upon himself, the idea being that he will soon lose the urge to buck when, each time he tries, he is met with this device. I do not intend to describe this in any more detail here, as neither I, nor Max, would wish anyone to try to make one.

Max tells me that since working with Andy Andrews, he has come to realise that the vast majority of horses that buck, do so because of pain, and it is normally possible to eradicate this pain. Although Max does not decry the use of this device, he has found, over the years, an armoury of other ways in which to approach the problem and help the horse to learn not to buck. It is now his preference not to use 'the gumline', but he would not condemn its use by other experienced trainers, in situations where it appears to be the last option.

When a horse has had a serious problem, such as back pain causing him to buck, Max advises that after the source of the pain has been eradicated, it will be

'the horse should be urged on in gallop to overdose on his own pleasure'

necessary to go back to basic schooling. The horse needs to be given time to realise that the pain is not going to recur. Much time and patience is required for this process, and no two horses will react in exactly the same way.

Other Ridden Problems

Max also gives sound advice regarding such problems as jogging, jumping refusal, and rushing at fences. His advice here seems to me to be sensible, conventional, and in keeping with classical principles.

Reverse Psychology

He advocates the use of reverse psychology in some circumstances. An instance of this would be a horse who continually stops in front of his fences without a valid reason (pain, discomfort, bad riding). Max's advice here is, instead of harshly driving him forwards, which is probably what has happened in the past, ride the horse to the fence and ask him to stop in front of it. After some time of this decision being taken by the rider not to jump, the horse will then be keen to actually jump. I can well imagine how this could work; in the horse's mind, he is no longer getting his own way and gaining control and gets fed up with being asked to halt. In addition, this method is without the usual harshness that occurs in this type of situation.

This psychology is also advocated for such problems as a horse who continually pulls or runs away. Max advises that the rider takes the horse to a safe place, say a racing gallop, and gives with the reins. The horse then has nothing to pull against. The rider should let him gallop and, when he has had enough, he should be urged on to 'overdose on his own pleasure'. This is a fairly well-known piece of psychology, which I have used for many years with some success.

Another use for reverse psychology is for the horse who rushes backwards. Yes, you've guessed it, you ask him to rein-back over long distances until he is thoroughly fed up with going backwards. Obviously, the place for this schooling has to be well chosen from the safety aspect. A public road would definitely not be the place.

Reverse psychology is not new, but some of the ways in which Max applies it do make good sense.

Biting

Since writing *Understanding Your Horse*, Max's views on biting have slightly altered. He now believes that everyday riders should not deal with serious biters; they are far too dangerous. The owner of a serious biter should seek professional help, since it takes a great deal of experience to know when to stand your ground or when to back off, and you make the wrong decision at your peril.

However, many horses are not serious about their biting and are what may be described as 'nippers'. In this instance, Max says that you must refrain from punishing the horse, as this will only make matters worse. Although it is a normal reaction to want to lash out if a horse bites, you must stop yourself. Max believes that horses usually bite for two reasons. The first of these reasons is pain – obviously the source of pain must be sought out and eradicated, then the problem should cease. The second common reason is that the horse has a lack of respect for the trainer/handler. In this case, you should go back to plenty of groundwork, making sure that the horse respects your space and will move freely forwards, backwards or sideways if asked. This work may take some time to show an improvement, but the horse's behaviour should improve in the course of time.

QUESTION 1: *Are there any horses with which you would not use join-up?*

MAX'S REPLY: In the past, Monty Roberts has not been afforded the luxury of having time to spend on problem horses to enable him to gain a trusting relationship, and he has always had to prove and re-prove his methods, so in that way join-up has been necessary. If you need quick results it definitely works, but as a rule I try to avoid using it on horses who have been abused or that are fairly wild, as they have a very strong flight instinct, so they will just run and run to exhaustion and that is not what I want. So, with the really traumatized horse, I like if possible to get close to them and get a more personal relationship with them and take more time. I think that join-up has to be a part of the process at some point, but I find that with very traumatized horses it is not the most prudent first step. Sometimes, however, there are occasions when join-up may be the best first step, as an alternative may be worse. You cannot be rigid, always keep an open mind to the best thing for that particular horse in that situation.

QUESTION 2: *Do you consider that it is desirable to use join-up on horses who are already well bonded with their owners/handlers?*

MAX'S REPLY: If you have a great relationship with your horse, there is no real need to use join-up. My attitude here is: if it isn't broke, don't fix it. A lot of people have been bitterly disappointed. After coming to a demonstration, they go home and try join-up on their own horse. The trouble is that they probably didn't have a full enough understanding of the advance-and-retreat method and didn't fully appreciate what join-up is all about. In this way, they have really upset their horse and, understandably, become quite upset themselves. My advice is to leave well alone if you have a good relationship, and only use join-up if you are sure you understand the principles.

QUESTION 3: *I believe that you are not in favour of traditional lungeing, but what type of lungeing, if any, do you use?*

MAX'S REPLY: About three or four years ago, people started to say to me 'we love your demonstrations, but we don't have a round pen'. If a loading problem comes in to me, I would spend two or three days in the round pen, joining-up and doing halter work, before dealing with the issue of loading, so most of the horses are very obedient and happy to follow before loading commences. When I go out to problem horses and there is no round pen, I would start with halter work such as moving the quarters away. Most of the horses who have loading problems also have other handling issues, and after about five minutes of halter work, would decide they were going to leave! Being on a 20 foot (7m) rope, they would go out and start circling. After a while, they would realise that going round on a circle was actually hard work. I found that, as in join-up, there came a point when they were ready to take the option of coming back in when invited. I then started to use this process when going out to do horses where there was no round pen.

On one occasion, I was using this process on a lady's horse, and she told me that my technique was similar to Pat Parelli's. At that time, I had never seen Pat Parelli working, so I went to see what he does. I found that some of his techniques made a lot of sense. I have therefore incorporated some of these into my methods. I believe that it is silly to be too 'purist' in any sphere, and I like to take what suits me and the horse I am working with, from whatever source, whether it is my own idea or someone else's. I experimented with this technique and found that I could teach the horse to shift some of his weight from front to back and become more dextrous. I do this by asking the horse to come in and out on the circle using short turns on the hocks and turns on the forehand. I personally find lungeing round and round one way and then another for 30 minutes, quite mind numbing. I would say that my lungeing is a hybrid of Parelli circling work and conventional lungeing.

QUESTION 4: *What is your opinion of Parelli Natural Horsemanship?*

MAX'S REPLY: Some people are very quick to knock other training methods. When the same person has taught these people and they are all working with the same principles, if they put their counterparts down, then they are putting themselves down. I find this very silly and unnecessary. The 'grandfather' of this type of natural horsemanship was Tom Dorrance. If I find a better method than the one I am currently using, wherever it may come from, I will use it. This is what true horsemanship is all about – never being too proud to learn and keeping an open mind to other methods. I would question certain things used in Parelli Natural Horsemanship, but I probably do an incredible number of things which Parelli does. However, I do things in my own way and possibly do not take them so far. Pat Parelli is an amazing horseman, as is Monty Roberts. Sometimes the interpretation of their methods by their followers can go slightly awry. This is why I am a little cautious of that kind of thing myself. I think that Parelli Natural Horsemanship methods contain sound principles but, like anything, can be misconstrued and misused. I do use a lot of their principles, firstly without realising that I have been doing it. After speaking with Pat and watching him work I have come to admire him.

Most alternative or natural horsemanship methods contain so many common denominators. Sound horsemanship principles run right across the board, be it classical, alternative or whatever.

QUESTION 5: *With the onset of many new and 'natural' training techniques, and many charlatans undoubtedly 'jumping on the bandwagon', do you think that we are in danger of becoming 'naturally' obsessed, where anything that goes by the name 'natural' is followed and revered whether it is good or bad?*

MAX'S REPLY: Yes, definitely. I feel that when Monty Roberts came to the UK nearly 15 years ago, it opened up the floodgates for a lot of people to see things a little differently. I certainly changed a lot of what I was doing at that time and got slightly sucked into the 'natural' culture. I realised that I was starting to forget about true, sound principles. There is an element where people have become too natural. We have to realise that even putting a horse in a field is not a natural environment for it. It massages our conscience, but we cannot treat our horses totally 'naturally' if we want to own them and ride them. We have to make compromises and compensate for what we have taken away from horses.

'people who believe we should not use antibiotics or put metal shoes on horses are 'natural' to the ridiculous'

Any kind of bit can be a wonderful tool in the right hands and an instrument of torture in the hands of someone with no feel or tact. That does not mean that we should all ride in bitless bridles – although bitless bridles do have their place in certain circumstances. People who believe that we should never use antibiotics and not put metal shoes on horses are 'natural' to the ridiculous. It would be marvellous if every horse could work without shoes, but this is not the case. It would be lovely if we had herbal remedies to cure everything, but that also is not the case. We should all try to keep a balance in what we do with our horses and make judgements according to the particular horse and situation.

QUESTION 6: *I believe that you admire the work of Sylvia Loch and the Classical Riding Club. Do you have the chance to practise classical riding techniques or are you at present too busy sorting out the many poor abused horses that come into your care?*

MAX'S REPLY: I do admire Sylvia Loch and the Classical Riding Club, but the past ten years for me has been purely sorting out problem horses. The precious intervals in between times have been when someone sends me a youngster to be backed. However, the rearers, buckers, and napping horses have all taught me classical principles, without me going to a classical trainer. They have taught me the importance of straightness, rhythm, engagement and cadence. When you have all of those things, then self-carriage is a natural by-product. I have been taught by the difficult horses who have had conventional 'bully-boy' tactics used upon them, and this has failed time and time again. I have been taught by these horses how to consider classical principles such as 'do I need more control of the shoulder with this horse or should I concentrate on lateral work, to help it to become more straight?'

I have studied the writings of Nuño Oliveira. I also came to the realisation, when working with Monty, that good western riding is very akin to classical training. Classical training emerged from the practice of training horses for war, to fight in the bull-ring and to work cattle. The problem horses are stuck in the middle, which made it necessary for me to think more classically.

QUESTION 7: *What do you think of the competitive equestrian scene, in terms of welfare of the horse as well as standard of riding?*

MAX'S REPLY: Dreadful – right across the board. The only discipline where I find it a little better is in eventing. This is not a bias because I have evented, but I do feel that event riders seem to have a little more empathy with their horses. This could be because, when you are galloping towards solid fences at 30 mph, if you do not have a rapport with your horse, then it is only a matter of time before you have a bad accident. In the UK, we have some of the best horses in the world, and we complain about our lack of success on an international scale. However, the riding standard in this country has become deplorable. The judging standard is just as bad to allow this to happen.

QUESTION 8: *Do you think that the quality of life for horses in general, in most parts of the world, is improving?*

MAX'S REPLY: Yes, definitely so in the developed countries, such as the UK, Europe, North America, South Africa, Australia and so on. However, you only have to go to somewhere such as Egypt to see that nothing has changed.

QUESTION 9: *Apart from the obviously huge influence of Monty Roberts are there any other trainers or methods that you have come across over the years which still influence you?*

MAX'S REPLY: Andy Andrews, as you have already mentioned, has been a huge influence on me. He really affected my thinking on problem horses, making me realise that the vast majority of them are in pain, rather than just a proportion of them as I had previously believed.

As a kid, my hero in show jumping was Eddie Macken with Boomerang. Eddie Macken's riding was second to none. He was a perfect, classical, show jumping rider, and I have tried to model my own riding on him. He always looked as though he could jump without saddle or bridle and it would make no difference. He sat perfectly still and calm, folding perfectly forward over the jump and coming gently back into the saddle on landing, without moving his leg position or interfering with the horse in any way. I admire people who are good horsemen, in whatever discipline, whether it is dressage, show jumping or eventing. Mark Todd in eventing, always looks a part of the horse, and anyone who can do that will inspire me.

'the riding standard in the UK has become deplorable. The judging standard is just as bad to allow this to happen'

Summary and Conclusions

In keeping with other training methods, such as police-horse training, Max advises that horses should be desensitized to frightening things, such as vehicles, prams, umbrellas and so on, before they are taken out onto the road.

It seems to me that Richard Maxwell has utilized the Monty Roberts join-up methods and combined them with many other methods of conventional training. He is not against the sensible use of the whip, although he is totally against beating the horse into submission. He recognises that the rider/handler has to be the leader of the partnership between horse and human, and recommends that the human should hold 51 per cent of the power, with which I totally agree.

'draw reins and the like have absolutely no place in the training of horses'

Max is against any kind of bearing rein. Here is what he told me about draw reins:

'I believe that draw reins and the like have absolutely no place at all in the training of horses. I have seen so many horses with physiologically damaged necks caused by draw reins. Any equestrian tool, such as a whip, can be misused, but they can equally easily be used sensitively to help the horse. When it comes to draw reins, it is 95 per cent easier to misuse them, and you only have a 5 per cent chance of getting it right.'

This statement is like music to my ears! Fellow classical teachers, myself included, have been saying this for years, and it is nice to hear it confirmed from a different source.

The thing that most impresses me about Richard Maxwell is his open-mindedness and willingness to change his ideas and modify his methods if he finds something that is better (and to admit that he has changed). This, to me, is the epitome of a true horseman. To my mind, trainers who never admit to ever being wrong are completely foolhardy and blinkered. One of the attributes required of a true horseman is humility, and this is what is sadly lacking in many riders and trainers today. It is self-importance and a lack of humility which, to my mind, leads to the perpetuation of many questionable practices – no-one dares to question the validity of them for fear of becoming 'an outcast'. Gladly, this is definitely not the case with Richard Maxwell. He freely tells us that his methods are taken from various different sources, and that he will always use the best of whatever methods he can find that may help a specific horse.

Obviously, there are points here and there with which I disagree, but this is only to be expected. However, I fully agree with most aspects of Max's training. He does appear to have an understanding of weight aids, which of course have been advocated by good classical riders for hundreds of years, but which unfortunately some modern trainers totally ignore. In short, I would say that he has successfully married the new and old techniques, as well as incorporating his own ideas.

CHAPTER 5

GaWaNi
Pony Boy

The Horsemanship of the Native American Indians

'It is more important to concentrate on the
relationship between human and horse than it is
to concentrate on the required results'

Horse, Follow Closely

t may come as a surprise to many people that the Native American Indians have only had access to horses for a few hundred years. This time span could be compared with the blink of an eye, in comparison with the thousands of years in which the rest of the world has benefited from the horse. It is worthy of note, that in this short space of time, the American Indians have developed a remarkable rapport with their horses. It is even more remarkable when one remembers that much of this has been achieved without the benefit of the teachings of the great horsemasters available to most of the rest of the equestrian world.

Historians tell us, that as long as 40 million years ago, ancestors of the modern horse did exist in the Americas, but this was long before mankind existed. However, for some reason, along with many other species, they became extinct. It was the Spanish Conquistadors who brought the first horses, as we know them, to the American continent, in the late 16th century. These were Spanish Barb horses; they were small, around 14.2hh, stocky, and were known for their endurance and ability to fend for themselves. In the late 17th century, the French and English also brought horses to America. These were mainly heavy breeds such as the Suffolk Punch and the Percheron. Some of these horses inevitably became feral and interbred with the Barb. This inter-breeding formed the Mustang, which is now a breed in its own right. Most of the wild horses living in North America are not, strictly speaking, wild but feral; they are domesticated horses, which have escaped. Many of these feral horses have been living in the wild for only a generation or two.

'survival in battle depended on the relationship they had with their horse'

Once the Native Americans had domesticated horses, their world changed dramatically. Their horizons expanded – horses could easily travel 20 miles per day. They could hunt much larger prey, such as buffalo, and their hunting territories obviously expanded. Horses became extremely important animals to own. They were traded and highly prized. Many of the tribes created their own breeding programmes and utilized gelding practices, so that only the more desirable characteristics would be perpetuated. It was from one of these breeding programmes that the famous spotted Appaloosa horse originated.

One of the uses to which the Natives put their horses was, of course, to carry them into war. It was soon realised that their survival in battle may well depend on the relationship they had with their horse. The classical masters mirror this idea in many of the books. War, unfortunately, has nearly always played a huge part in human history bringing disaster and suffering, for horse and human alike, but at least it has made mankind think of the horse as a friend. Therefore, great emphasis was put upon the ability to communicate with the horse, and much time and effort was spent to this end. Many Native Americans considered that their horses had equal status to themselves, as 'brother-warriors'.

Much of the Native American ethos towards their horses is derived from their belief that all species on this earth are related. They had great respect for the prey animals that they were obliged to eat. There is much folklore amongst the tribes, which tells of medicine men who could communicate with animals. This ethos required them to be what we would now term as 'eco-friendly'. They did not kill for the sake of killing, and every part of the animal that had been killed would be used whenever possible. They had great respect for nature – something many of us in the modern world could benefit by attempting to emulate.

GaWaNi Pony Boy and Relationship Training®

It is difficult for us to fully understand, but the Native American religious culture has always taken the view that all creatures on earth (including humans) are brothers and sisters. Even rocks and plants were given respect, in the same way that a family member would be respected. This philosophy no doubt gave them a head start in the training of horses. They were not hampered by the human pride and desire for over-dominance, as so many of us are. They could approach their horses' training with a natural humility, that most of us in the western world have to work to achieve (provided we understand, in the first place, that we need it).

GaWaNi Pony Boy's work has been recognised over the years as a sensitive approach to horsemanship, mirroring those values held by Native American Indians. He enjoys a worldwide following, with his events and private evaluations attracting thousands of participants each year in the USA as well as abroad. Horses of all breeds and riders of all disciplines have benefited from his 'Horses Teaching People' approach to training. As he points out, horses were regarded as messengers, teachers or guides, rather than students. It is easy to see then, from this perspective, how they did not need to be told to listen to their horses.

As with every culture, religion, creed, nationality or association, the opposite of the above gentle approach to the world has no doubt been practised by some Native Americans. By this, I mean that there are many reports of extreme cruelty by some tribes towards their own tribal members, as well as acts of barbarism towards animals. However, this does not detract in my mind from the good intentions of the religious ethos of the Native Americans. Anyone who is tempted to be too judgemental should perhaps look at what goes on in some areas of our own society.

'horses were regarded as messengers, teachers or guides, rather than students ...'

In his book *Horse, Follow Closely* (BowTie Press 1998) GaWaNi Pony Boy points out that the Native Americans did not try to treat a horse in the same way as a dog – they knew that they were totally different. Because they already enjoyed such an awareness of animals and nature, they very quickly understood the personality of the horse. They therefore set out to train, ride and communicate with their horses using their knowledge of the nature of the animal. GaWaNi's approach to training is based on two basic points:

- It is necessary for the trainer to understand the boundaries and behaviours inherent in the horse's life as a herd animal.
- It is more important to concentrate on the relationship between human and horse than it is to concentrate on the required results.

Understanding of Psychology

The Indians obviously understood the horse's psychology, in terms of being a prey animal which is hunted and lives in large herds, as a means of self-preservation. This is a subject with which we are now being bombarded by many of the modern trainers, as if it is a new notion that has only just been discovered. To be fair, it may be that most of us do need to be reminded of these aspects. It must be born in mind, however, that the Native Americans have never forgotten them, and it is possible that their understanding of the horse's instinctive behaviour surpasses that of even the 'new' trainers of today.

Challenging the Leadership

GaWaNi reminds us that horses living in a herd are constantly challenging the leadership of higher-ranking animals. Thus, the most qualified horses are the ones who will stay in the leadership positions, and this will benefit the herd as a whole. It is at this point where GaWaNi's advice on how to remain the higher member of the 'two-person' herd seems, in my opinion, to be very similar to Monty Roberts's join-up technique:

'When you and your horse are standing in a training arena, your horse will usually first exhibit his leadership qualities by walking, or trotting, high-headed, around you. When you do not follow as he expects you to, he may begin to question his own position in the herd. He will begin to pay more attention to you by pivoting an ear toward you, or possibly turning to face you. Walk in front of your horse expecting him to follow, and he will.' (Horse, Follow Closely)

This is so similar to Monty Roberts's join-up, when he says that the horse will start to lower his head and tilt an ear towards the trainer when he is becoming ready to join-up. The main difference I can see is that Monty actually drives the horse away, using aggressive body language, to instigate the flight mechanism, whereas GaWaNi Pony Boy is not advocating any aggressive body language. He is merely suggesting an appropriate reaction from the trainer, when the horse has made his own choice to challenge the trainer for the dominant position. Monty Roberts no doubt does not have the luxury of being able to wait for the horse to make this choice. His situation is different and dictated by time. Nevertheless, it would seem that both the Native Americans and Monty Roberts have independently discovered this part of the horse's language.

Importance of Time

GaWaNi impresses on us that time is the most important tool in Relationship Training® with a horse. If we lived as closely with our horses as the Native Americans have done in the past, then I am sure that we would all have a deeper understanding of our equine friends. In most cases, the horses were left to share the meadows around the camp. They were neither hobbled, nor tied, nor fenced in. In other words, they chose to stay there. If a predator should approach during the night, the people in the camp were alerted by the noises from the horses. The young men would leave the tepees and drive the predator away. I would imagine that this must have put the human owners of these horses very high in the esteem of the horses, as good herd leaders and protectors.

'we should all take time, when possible, just to 'hang out' with our horses'

From the human perspective, this way of life gives the humans a far deeper understanding of the feelings, noises and body language exhibited by their horses, since they were witnessing this all the time. GaWaNi therefore insists that we should spend time with our horses – just being with them, observing them, and being part of their world. It is not good enough just to carry out tasks in their vicinity. This is a requirement that would be almost impossible to fulfil for the majority of today's busy horse owners. Nevertheless, maybe we should all take time, when possible, just to 'hang out' with our horses, even if it does mean missing that ride or not going to that show. Maybe we would benefit from a respite from the daily rush, as much as our horses would benefit from having us with them as he suggests in his book *Time Well Spent* (BowTie Press 1999).

Verbal, Physical and Focal Messages

GaWaNi, along with other trainers such as Monty Roberts and Pat Parelli, maintains that the horse's primary means of communication is by body language. However, he does not rule out the use of vocal commands, as many 'natural' trainers do. He advocates a combination of verbal, physical and focal messages. The vocal communication can be used to calm and soothe a horse. In addition, verbal commands are useful to convey a degree of urgency, in other words to avoid danger. Horses are well able to distinguish between varying degrees of the same message.

Perhaps the most neglected of these three means of communication (at least by many traditional training methods) is that of focus. Here again, we must not forget the focus of the true horseman. There is no doubt in my mind of the importance of focus. Have you ever intended to turn your horse, say to the right, but then something makes you focus to the left – and your horse hesitates because he senses that the physical and focal aids are in conflict? This may also, of course, have something to do with the direction in which you are turning your head, but I am sure that there is more to it than that. We have all had the feeling that someone is staring at us; we turn around to find that an old friend is trying to attract our attention. Horses are very good at homing in on riders' feelings, and when the Native Americans were in situations of heightened emotion, say during a buffalo hunt, then their horses' response to physical aids could be practically instant, when the focal aid had preceded it.

Bitting

GaWaNi's ideas on bitting are very straightforward; the bit should ideally be used only to reinforce verbal, physical and focal cues. His reasons for not using harsh bits are valid and, in my view, closely related to classical thinking – the difference being that a classical rider would develop gentle and sensitive hands, in order to communicate tactfully with his

'the bit should be used only to reinforce verbal, physical and focal cues'

horse. For this type of intimate communication between the rider's hands and the horse's mouth, it is often necessary to use a bit other than a mild snaffle, with which it is sometimes difficult to give delicate vibratory aids. However, bitting is a subject worthy of many books – past, present

and future. I will not, therefore, delve too deeply into this subject here. Suffice to say that the Native Americans seem to have a kind attitude towards bitting, albeit that they have come to this approach without the influence of the classical masters.

Use of a 'Switch'

Native Americans have traditionally used a 'switch', which is a braided leather short whip about two feet (60cm) long, as a training tool. The first half is made of plaited leather and the second half of loose pieces of soft leather. This switch was used as a reinforcement of a physical aid and as an encouragement – more as a pat on the back. This seems admirable to me – almost identical to the way in which true classical trainers use their whips.

The Halt

The Native American use of body aids to guide the horse to a halt, however, would seem almost the opposite to that of the classical aids. GaWaNi's advice to teach the horse to halt is to 'pull up your knees about six inches so they are resting just behind your horse's shoulder blades. As you do this, lean back from your hips and allow your backward motion to slowly bring the reins back with you.' (*Horse, Follow Closely*)

This would surely push the weight of the rider to the back of the seat bones and further back on the horse's back, thus making it difficult for the horse to come to a halt with a good back posture, and probably encouraging him to hollow his back. The classical way to come to a halt would be for the rider to advance the hips with an expanded chest and toned abdominal muscles, sit very tall, slightly bracing the spine, and, using a closing feel with the thighs and knees, keeping the lower leg on the horse just enough to encourage the back legs to support the halt. With practice, the halt can be executed in this manner without the need for reinforcement with the reins, although in the early stages, or when a fast response is required, a closing of the fingers on the reins should be all that is required to reinforce this aid.

The practice of advancing the hips is a very natural thing. Just try walking yourself, put your hands on your hips and stop. You will feel how natural it is for your hips to advance.

What feels natural to the rider will generally feel natural to the horse. However, it must be said that I am writing this with the benefit of learning from the great masters, whose knowledge has been collected throughout thousands of years.

For more in-depth information on body posture, I suggest you read Sylvia Loch's books. A good place to start would be *The Classical Seat* (A Horse and Rider Publication 1988) and *Invisible Riding* (DJ Murphy (Publisher) Ltd 2003). The Native Americans did not have this benefit.

Use of Rewards

The Native American elders teach that when a horse does something well, or when he has tried hard, he should be rewarded with pats, hugs and kind words. These are regular parts of Relationship Training® as they are in traditional training. It is refreshing to hear this sound, and kind, commonsense, coming from a method of training that is based so fundamentally on a 'natural' basis. Many of the modern, so-called 'natural', trainers tell us that horses do not appreciate this type of reward. GaWaNi very wisely warns of the dangers of using these treats as bribes – wait until the horse has at least tried to do something right.

Riding Bareback

GaWaNi advises that all riders should ride bareback for at least two months. He says that once a healthy relationship has been established, it is perfectly acceptable for a saddle to be introduced. I believe that it is during this time of riding bareback that most Native Americans develop their balance and become, unknowingly, very similar to good classical riders. GaWaNi talks of adjusting your centre of balance and to avoid hanging on with the legs. In this way, you would, of necessity, be sitting just behind where the withers start to rise and be utilizing the laws of gravity as nature intended. Sylvia Loch advises:

'all riders should ride bareback for at least two months'

'It is only when the rider has sufficient suppleness and balance to drop their weight down over the horse's centre of motion, which happens also to be the horse's strongest point, around the fourteenth vertebra, that the rider can achieve that magical state when they unite their balance with that of the horse.' (*The Classical Rider* JA Allen 1997)

Around the fourteenth vertebra is where the ribs are at their longest and usually puts the rider just behind the withers. This is why so many classical trainers warn against allowing the seat to slide backwards, thereby putting weight onto the horse's loins – the weakest part of the back. I would add a word of warning here.

When fitting a saddle, while bearing in mind that the strongest part of the horse's back is normally slightly behind the withers, one must also be mindful of the fact that the saddle should be far enough back so as not to interfere with the movement of the shoulders. It is impossible to give an absolutely definitive optimum position for the saddle,

because of the vast differences in conformation of types and breeds of horses.

The illustration shows a stylized statue of Simon Bolivar, who was born in Caracas in 1783. He was one of the Spanish settlers and a soldier in the Conquistador army. Most authorities believe that it was the Conquistador's style of riding which influenced the Native Americans, once they had acquired their own horses. This riding position is typical of the classical riding style of the Americas at that time, as introduced by the Spanish.

While it is true that many old engravings show people riding bareback and sitting well back on the horse's loins, this was later recognised to be harmful to the horse. In his book *The Art of Horsemanship,* Xenophon wrote: 'I do not approve of a seat which is as though the man were on a chair but rather as though he were standing upright with his legs apart…His foot and leg from the knee down should hang loosely.'

GaWaNi's description of how and where to sit on the horse would therefore seem to be in unison with classical teaching. I find it amazing when I consider the extent to which the Native American horsemanship echoes that of the classical school. Equally amazing is the fact that they apparently modified this dressage-type seat to a more forward seat for faster riding over rough ground, similar to that used by good race jockeys today. They seem to know instinctively where the centre of gravity lies and that it needs to change when the horse changes pace.

I am impressed by GaWaNi's awareness of the importance of the saddle fitting the horse correctly, and how the horse can change shape due to weight, age, muscle and so on, and may need a change of saddle accordingly. He strongly advises against using a bareback pad, which he says is an English-saddle-shaped piece of fleece or wool with a girth. Some have handles at the pommel, and some even have stirrups. GaWaNi warns that they can be extremely dangerous, as they can easily slide around. I would have thought that, being without a gullet, they could also cause spinal pressure on the horse – certainly a good enough reason not to use one!

Exercise One – Spending a day with the horse

The first exercise we are advised to carry out in Relationship Training® is to spend a day with our horse.

Exercise Two – Familiarization with training tools

The second exercise is to familiarize the horse to the training tools with which we will be working. This is somewhat similar to the 'Friendly Game' advocated by Pat Parelli (see page 81). GaWaNi describes how to run your hands all over your horse's body and to identify the sensitive areas. Once you know which areas are sensitive, he advises us to focus on them, caress them gently, but, when the horse becomes too upset, to retreat and continue stroking, say on the neck, very gradually and gently returning to the sensitive areas. Once the horse is comfortable with your hands touching all over him, then we are advised to do the same with the tools, starting with the switch. Touch or gently brush all over with the switch, until your horse is comfortable with being touched by each piece of equipment. This exercise should need to be done only once at the initial stage of training. However, if the horse shows fears of any particular tool, then the exercise can be reinforced at any stage.

Exercise Three – Teaching the horse to come

The third exercise in Relationship Training® is to teach the horse to come towards the trainer and to halt when asked. I particularly liked this very sensible and gentle approach. Although there is a similarity in the Parelli system, in other words the 'Yo-Yo Game' (see page 81), I found GaWaNi's approach, from the horse's point of view, totally different. His advice is to use an eight-foot (2.5m) lead rope and, facing the horse while holding the rope about one foot (30cm) from the horse's nose, take three or four backwards steps. Do not pull on the rope, but make soft eye contact with him. As soon as the horse starts to make a step towards you, praise him. Give him a moment to understand what has happened and do the exercise again. Most horses will soon understand and follow you with your first step backwards.

The next phase is to teach your horse to stop once he has started to follow you. You should start by walking backwards as before. When he starts following you, walk a few more steps, and then stop abruptly. As soon as the horse begins to stop, you should reward him immediately. He also advises us to do the same exercises again using sideways steps – always using the same reward sequence. This is where the difference is most noticeable. GaWaNi's approach is one of positive reward when the horse does what is required. There is no aggressive driving away and then cessation when the horse does what is required – which, to my mind, is just the lesser of two evils from the horse's point of view. With a positive-reward system, the horse is most likely to remain relaxed and to step away smoothly without throwing his head in the air and hollowing his back, which could, in my opinion, be detrimental to him.

'GaWaNi's approach is one of positive reward when the horse does what is required'

To teach the horse to stop, GaWaNi advises us to use focal impression and body language, but not aggressiveness. When you back away from your horse, change your focus from coaxing to a feel of distancing yourself from your horse. When your horse begins to follow, you should take a step towards him and ask him to stop. The horse should not be rewarded at this point, but neither should he be punished. If he begins to follow and then hesitates, you should immediately reward him. It is easy to imagine that, using this method with time and patience, the horse will learn what is required without any stress. The object is to increase the time that the horse will stand until asked to move towards you again. When you are asking your horse to stand, GaWaNi advises that we should avoid eye contact. We should again make soft eye contact when we want him to approach us.

This point is interesting since in describing his join-up method, Monty Roberts says the exact opposite; in other words that direct eye contact is a sign of dominance. Monty advises that you should drop your head and avoid eye contact when you wish your horse to follow you for 'follow-up'. My own theory on this point is that neither Monty Roberts nor the Native Americans have misinterpreted the equine language. Both of these techniques work in different situations. I believe that it is the 'type' of eye contact that matters and differs; in other words whether there is an aggressive look in the eye or, as described by GaWaNi, a soft eye contact. I am sure every horse owner will remember seeing a particular look in their horse's eye, say an aggressive look before the ears are laid back, or a soft, tender, look just before a gentle nuzzle. I am sure that horses are just as able to read facial expressions as we are, and probably are a lot better at it!

Exercise Four – Mounting

In this exercise devoted to mounting GaWaNi again looks at life through the horse's eyes. He wants us to be able to mount without compromising the horse's balance. He describes, in great detail, how to vault on from the ground, placing your seat on the horse's back gracefully in one fluid movement. Strangely enough, this is exactly the way that I used to mount as I child, when riding bareback as I often did. I have to confess that I

'we should be able to mount without compromising the horse's balance'

don't think I could do it now! Nevertheless, I do fully agree that we should make mounting a less disturbing movement for the horse. The best compromise I can make is to use a mounting block and ask someone to hold the opposite stirrup, thereby keeping the saddle firmly in place without it rocking on the poor horse's back.

Exercise Five – Developing focal skills while mounted

This is devoted to developing your focal skills while mounted. GaWaNi describes in detail not only how the rider should focus himself, but also how to read the signs of the horse focusing on the rider and his wishes. He maintains that physical cues should be used only to reinforce focal ones.

Exercise Six – Reinforcement of focal cues with physical cues

This is devoted to the reinforcement of focal cues with physical cues, or – as we know them – aids. GaWaNi does not advocate driving a horse away from a certain direction, say with pressure from one leg, but prefers to think of leading the horse into the required direction. This philosophy is in contradiction to classical riding methods. However, he goes on to describe how to shift your weight slightly to one side, and the horse will move under that weight in order to re-establish natural balance. This is an exact replica of classical principles, as passed down by the great masters. I find it admirable that people such as the

'the horse and rider's centre of gravity is constantly changing while in motion'

Native Americans have discovered this principle, without recourse to the European equestrian world. They obviously understood, from the word go, the laws of gravity and the fact that the horse and rider's centre of gravity is constantly changing while in motion.

GaWaNi goes on to explain how to ask the horse to move, circle, back up, and so on, by using focal cues and changing the centre of gravity. All this is done without kicking and without pulling on the horse's mouth.

Exercise Seven – Falling off

This is an aspect of riding that is all too often neglected. Not many of us want to think of the prospect of a possible fall, and especially not as we get older and a little stiffer. However, I do feel that it would benefit young riders in particular, if they could have a basic idea of what to do and when to do it, if the time should arrive when they are heading for a fall. How many broken limbs could be avoided if we knew how to roll when we fall, instead of putting out our arms? GaWaNi gives very concise and good advice. I just hope that people practising this use soft material to land on and have a helper on hand.

Exercise Eight – Verbal cues

GaWaNi thinks that we should limit our verbal commands when riding, but he certainly advocates using them in certain circumstances. His advice seems very logical and consistent with good horsemanship.

Exercise Nine – Jumping

GaWaNi's approach to jumping seems to me very much the same as any good conventional jumping trainer. Jumping is approached, like everything else in *Horse, Follow Closely*, with empathy for the horse's viewpoint. Jumps are at first very low and gradually built up, while building the horse and rider's confidence. The main difference is that he is able to jump bareback, although he does not insist that this is essential, and certainly should not be attempted until an advanced degree of expertise has been reached in the other exercises.

Exercise Ten – The obstacle course

GaWaNi describes how to close a training session with a mini obstacle course, which should be approached with a light-hearted attitude and is designed to be fun for the horse. It could consist of a course of varied manoeuvres such as cone slaloms, small jumps or ground poles, turns, circles and so on. This sounds like a good way to keep the horse's interest and also to improve the relationship between horse and rider, providing the horse does genuinely enjoy the course.

Exercise Eleven – Night riding

This is an idea that is quite new to me. Apart from police horses, who have to patrol at night, not many people actually train at night without the aid of artificial light. GaWaNi suggests that you first choose a moonlit night, for obvious reasons! The object of this exercise is to practice and reinforce your focal cues. I can well imagine how 'at one' the

'bucking is normally a response to pain or fear'

Native Americans must feel when able to ride in the dark with no fear – both horse and rider having complete trust in one another. GaWaNi does, very sensibly, advise that if you are not comfortable with riding at night, then do not do it. Obviously, the object is to enhance the trust and bond between horse and rider, and fear on the rider's part could destroy it.

At the end of *Horse, Follow Closely* GaWaNi reiterates how horses in the herd situation are constantly challenging other herd members, and the herd leader constantly has to reassert his position. This is a concept that is widely accepted by other trainers. It is only natural, therefore, that the horse will occasionally test his human herd leader by aggressive moves. GaWaNi advises us to deal with such attempts at dominance in the same way as an equine leader would – with a short, sharp reprimand. For instance, a bite could be met with a sharp slap and a short, loud yell. He explains that although kicking is very dangerous to humans, it is not normally intended to be so dangerously aggressive in the horse's mind as we might think. He advises that although we should not tolerate kicking, we should not deal with it in the same way as biting, as it may provoke another kick. We could try raising the offending leg, as when picking the foot out, and holding it up for a few minutes. As this is a mildly uncomfortable position, it is usually enough to give the message to the horse that kicking is not acceptable. GaWaNi is very aware that bucking is normally a response to pain or fear and should not be punished. The trainer should seek the source of such fear or pain, or otherwise return to basic Relationship Training®.

Lungeing

It is very refreshing to hear a 'natural' trainer who not only approves of lungeing in its purest form, but actually admires the art. He says that it should be a way of training a horse to respond to physical and verbal aids. I could not agree more, however, that in many cases lungeing deteriorates into a mindless exercise with the horse running round in endless circles, which is obviously harmful. Lungeing should not be used as a means of punishment or reprimand. The horse will not understand this, and it will not make for a good relationship.

Summary and Conclusions

GaWaNi Pony Boy is of mixed-race Native American decent, and the horsemanship described in *Horse, Follow Closely* has been derived from the methods learned from the elders of different Native American nations. I expect that some of the ideas are his own, but the philosophy and main aspects originate from tribe elders. The general ethos and empathy with the horse is touching and has definite similarities to the teachings of the great classical masters. Other trainers, such as Monty Roberts and Pat Parelli reiterate certain aspects of the understanding of horse psychology and interaction within the herd situation.

I was impressed by the commonsense interpretation and way of dealing with the horse, without the use of either force or any kind of threat, but simply positive reinforcement; in other words, rewarding the horse when he does well. He is neither rewarded nor reprimanded when he does not do as required, unless he offers aggression to the trainer. This approach seems to me to be identical to the best of traditional training methods. The horse is not placed in an uncomfortable position and given a choice of two options, doing what the trainer requires being the lesser of two evils. It is actually made pleasant and enjoyable to do what is required, and therefore the horse will remain relaxed and learning will be easier.

'it is easy to image that, using this method with time and patience, the horse will learn what is required without stress'

CHAPTER 6

Pat Parelli

Speaking the Horse's Language

*'Horses don't care how much we know until they
know how much we care'*

During the past ten years, Parelli Natural Horsemanship has enjoyed almost world-wide fame and has become extremely popular in the UK, becoming almost as well known now as Monty Roberts' methods. At the Equus Event in London's Docklands in the spring of 2002, Neil Pye, an Australian who is currently the University Dean and a 5* Instructor at Pat's International Savvy Study Centers in Colorado and Florida, gave a demonstration and talk. The Parelli system has been developed over a period of 20 years, he explained, and it is currently the fastest growing equine training system.

Pat Parelli has, like Monty, trained a number of pupils who are now practising and teaching his methods in the UK. Supporters of the Parelli approach maintain that it is helpful for any type of riding and is not primarily Western.

'poor visual depth perception is the reason why a horse will shy at a puddle in the road'

US three-day event riders David and Karen O'Connor are perhaps Parelli's most well known advocates. Any horse can benefit from the Parelli approach, says Pat, not just problem horses.

Parelli Natural Horsemanship produce a series of audio tapes called *Understanding Natural Horsemanship*, in which Pat Parelli gives an in-depth explanation of his methods of training and the philosophies behind them. Most of his principles are excellent. Although many of them are not necessarily new, they are nevertheless very valid and are clearly explained. The following synopsis of my understanding of the principles of Parelli Natural Horsemanship is based largely on audio tapes, a series of video tapes, Pat's own documentation as well as live demonstrations on several occasions given by Neil Pye.

Thinking Like a Horse

Many different trainers often say that we should try to look at things from the horse's viewpoint. Pat Parelli asks us to imagine being out at night, without a torch or street-lights. When we hear a rustling sound, we are not sure whether anyone is there. Pat points out that this must be what the world is like, most of the time, for a horse. Most people realise that horses are prey animals with eyes on the side of the head, (as opposed to being predators with forward-facing eyes), and therefore have good peripheral vision, to the side and behind them. However, many people do not actually realise that this also means that they have poor visual depth perception. Poor visual depth perception is the reason why a horse will shy at a puddle in the road; he literally cannot tell that it may be only a quarter of an inch deep. As far as he can see, it could be six feet deep. Pat goes on to point out that some things, such as painted lines on the road, can be very confusing for a horse. We humans, on the other hand, are predators and cannot see to the side or behind us, but we have excellent depth perception – vital for homing in on a kill.

Pat also tells us things, which perhaps are quite obvious when we think about it, but the importance of which are often forgotten, such as the fact that prey animals smell like prey animals – horses smell of what they eat, in other words mainly grasses. As predators, humans smell mostly of meat. I had to smile with tongue in cheek here, because I have been a vegetarian for about 50 years. Does this mean that I have a head start when winning the confidence of a horse? I do hope so! Seriously, I do feel that this is a valid point, since horses have an excellent sense of smell, and I have often wondered whether they find our artificial perfumes offensive.

The age-old problem of the plastic bag spooking a horse is because this rustling sound is very much like a predator sneaking through the undergrowth. We are told that horses have three basic instincts:

- Perception of danger
- Flight
- To be gregarious – always wanting to be with the herd. They always have a consciousness of the whereabouts of 'home' or other horses

Pat's observation is that we differ from horses in that our priorities are praise, recognition and material possessions, whereas those of a horse are safety, comfort and play. In order to overcome these differences we are told that we have to work to close the relationship (prey–predator) gap, as Pat points out: 'Horses don't care how much we know until they know how much we care'.

Developing the Thinking Part of the Brain

Pat goes on to explain that the right side of the brain governs the horse's instinctive (prey animal) reaction, while the left side is responsible for the logical, thinking part of his behaviour. We therefore need to encourage him to be more 'left brained' – to use it more – and the way to do this is to make him comfortable. Rhythmic stroking, or using the 'Friendly Game', as described on page 81, will help achieve this.

Becoming the Alpha

Horses play dominance games all the time. They check out the hierarchy of the herd or field companions, trying all the time to increase their own status. Pat maintains that they will do this with humans as well. By learning the 'language' of the horse, and literally using the same games that horses use to establish friendship and dominance in the natural herd environment, we can become our horse's alpha – earning the respect that goes with it. Through playing the Seven Games – and winning them – we are using the same strategies that horses do, rather than aggression, force or intimidation, Pat maintains. Horses are natural followers, looking for natural leaders, and under good leadership they lose their fear, and become calmer, more confident and responsive.

Not Being a Predator

We can control the horse's movements, Pat says, by what he calls 'reverse psychology', in other words by making it comfortable for the horse to do as we wish, and uncomfortable if he does not. We can reward by easing the discomfort when he does as we desire. He says that we must use this reward very quickly – as soon as the horse makes the least little effort to do as we have asked – but that we should use few verbal commands. (In the Parelli System you are encouraged to rely less on verbal commands and instead use body and eye communication in a gentle and quiet way.)

Pat gives the very helpful advice of learning to have hands, and legs for that matter, that close slowly and open quickly. He explains that this is the opposite to the natural instinct of a predator, which is to close quickly and open slowly, particularly in a crisis situation. This is something on which we need to work. We should try to have a positive, relaxed reaction when the horse has a negative reaction, for example spooking at something. Pat maintains that he does not want to 'overtrain' his horses or risk them becoming 'roboticized'.

Areas of Savvy

'we need to have hands and legs that close slowly and open quickly…'

There are four areas of what Pat calls 'Savvy'. His definition of Savvy is knowing how to relate to horses, how to handle them, how to solve and prevent problems both on the ground and on the horse's back in any situation at any time. The four areas of Savvy include two on the ground and two mounted:

The No. 1 Savvy (On Line) is on the ground to get the horse to respond with respect when on the lead rope. We should not hold the horse close to the clip, but have a loose lead rope, to train the horse to follow the lead rope and also to go away from it. This is explained further in the Seven Games described on page 80.

The No. 2 Savvy (Liberty) is on the ground with the horse at liberty (not on a lead rope).

The No. 3 Savvy (Freestyle) is mounted, what he calls freestyle riding, with varying degrees of rein-use depending on the level. This, according to Parelli principles, prepares the horse for self-carriage and a sense of responsibility as well as an independent seat for the rider. We are told that horses and humans are prepared for riding with finesse with this No. 3 Savvy, and more athletic ability is engendered in the horse.

The No. 4 Savvy (Finesse) is mounted, with reins and focuses on contact and lightness in all areas of riding, with the ultimate goal being mental, physical and emotional collection in horse and rider.

Levels of the Savvy System

Pat maintains that his programme is primarily about self-development, and that the first three levels are designed specifically to teach the human and can be studied through the 'Savvy System' home-study format. Beyond Level 3, the programme is more about teaching the horse – performance horses, difficult horses, starting youngsters and so on – and intense hands-on teaching becomes essential.

Level 1: Partnership is about safety and confidence, and is underpinned by the Seven Games to break down the prey–predator barrier and to create a language with which to communicate with the horse. Both mounted work and work on the ground are involved.

Level 2: Harmony is about impulsion and positive reflexes to improve feel and timing, and branches into the four Savvys – On Line, Liberty, FreeStyle and Finesse.

'do not let your goals come before your principles'

Level 3: Refinement is underpinned by respect, impulsion, and flexion, and explores the development of vertical flexion for increased power through engagement of the hindquarters, once again using all four Savvys.

Level 4: Versatility is for those with professional goals, or for the extremely focused individual pursuing higher goals. The focus is on horsemanship and different horses, including young, difficult and performance horses. Personal tuition with either Pat Parelli or his top instructors is essential.

Above Versatility Level, there are higher levels, progressing through **Level 5 Unity**, **Level 6 True Unity**, **Levels 7, 8 and 9 Mastering True Unity**, to **Level 10 Ultimate Unity**.

While much of the Savvy System makes sense, I have some concerns over the first three levels being available in a home-study format – particularly as Pat says that no previous horse-riding experience is necessary for Level 1. It is also possible for students to 'self-assess' as they progress through the first three levels of the Savvy System, by utilizing the checklists and tasks for each lesson. Even with experienced horsemen, there is the potential – as with any new technique – for the Seven Games to be played incorrectly, with aggressive body language and a stressed horse as a result (neither of which are desired by Pat).

Training and supervision by Parelli instructors would ensure that students learned the games correctly, as intended by Pat Parelli. The instructors, who have passed rigorous and extensive testing (often taking years) before becoming endorsed, are available throughout the world for instruction. Intensive courses for all levels of horsemanship are available at both the Colorado and Florida (USA) Parelli International Study Centers, as well as other international centres, helping students to accelerate their learning. An 'official assessment' can be carried out either in a live session with a Parelli instructor, or via a video tape sent to an instructor. With any documentation published by any trainer, there is of course the potential for novice riders to 'go it alone' with unfortunate consequences. However, in my view, Parelli students – regardless of their level within the Savvy System – should be urged to seek advice and training from Parelli instructors, although of course then doing background reading and watching the videos would be invaluable.

Six Keys to Natural Training

Pat maintains that an unnatural way of training would be with fear, draw reins, drop nosebands, and so on. He says that there are six keys to natural training:

1 Attitude
Try to be positive – stay left brained. Smile on the inside and outside. Be realistic but positive. Do not let your goals come before your principles.

2 Knowledge
Make sure your knowledge matches up to the facts. Read more; take time to understand the theory.

3 Tools
There are tools for communication and tools for intimidation. Choose tools that will help you to put pressure on slowly and take it away quickly; eg leather-braided reins will not release quickly. Pat uses a double-woven rope for a quicker release.

4 Technique
It is scientifically proven, maintains Pat, that kicking the horse's sides does not speed a horse up, but increases the height of the stride. To ask for forward movement, we should squeeze or hug with the heels, tighten up the buttocks and turn the toes out. To make a downward transition, we are told to lift the reins up into the air and hold them there for a few seconds. If that does not work, then slowly turn the horse's head towards your knee.

The horse should be pushed into a turn; we are told not to lean or pull in the direction we are going. He asks us to put our weight onto our left foot when standing on the ground and then try to turn left – this cannot be done. We must therefore free up the weight from the inside leg.

This instruction seems to me to be a little confusing. The classical masters also tell us not to lean or pull the horse in the direction we wish to go, but the idea of taking weight away from the direction in which we are turning would seem to be contrary to the their teachings. Leaning is not at all the same thing as the transference of weight. This is what Col. Podhajsky has to say in his book *The Complete Training of Horse and Rider* (George G. Harrap

'there are tools for communication and tools for intimidation'

& Co. Ltd 1967): 'When the weight of the body is transferred into the direction of the lateral movement, it will support the effect of the outside leg because the horse will try to step under the centre of gravity of the rider.' Although he is referring to lateral movements here, it is obvious that the same principle applies to turning the horse – it is a simple law of nature.

When referring to the turn on the forehand, Waldemar Seunig writes in his book *Horsemanship* (Doubleday 1974): 'We stop in the middle of the riding hall, place additional load on the inner seat bone...'

General Decarpentry in his book *Academic Equitation* (JA Allen 1971) writes: 'The rider displaces the centre of gravity of the mass of Horse/Rider by altering his own position...In lateral movement, the best manner in which the rider can conform to these conditions, is by putting his weight on the stirrup that is on the side of the displacement.'

Finally, on this subject, Francois Robichon de la Guérinière wrote in his *Ecole de Cavalierie* in 1733: 'The aid of putting weight onto the stirrups is the subtlest of all the aids...by the mere act of putting more weight on one stirrup than the other, a horse is brought to respond to this movement.'

Pat Parelli tells us that there are two types of bits: those with shanks and those without.

'the focus of the eye is very important – we need to learn to look where we want to go'

Bits with shanks are made for riding with one hand and/or vertical flexion. Bits with no shanks, such as the snaffle bit, are made for using one rein at a time. We should carry out pre-ride checks before mounting, by using the Seven Games as described below.

We can use what he calls a 'carrot stick' to push the horse away. The carrot stick is four feet long, made of fibreglass, and has leather on one end. You can stand back from the horse and use this stick to rub him (the Friendly Game). We must make sure that the horse is 'left brained' before mounting.

The focus of the eyes is very important – we need to learn to look where we want to go, without allowing our eyes to stray.

We need to develop an independent seat, so that we do not need to use legs or reins to help us balance. To do this, we should ride bareback, possibly with a bareback pad or maybe without stirrups. We should also practise things such as standing on one leg when putting on our boots; trampolining or sports that may help our balance would also be good.

5 Time

We need to utilize our time better, if we do not have more time to spend. Allow the horse to tell us when he is ready to go on to the next level.

6 Imagination

Albert Einstein said that 'Imagination is even more valuable than knowledge'. Do what feels right for you and your horse, says Pat.

The Seven Games

In the *Seven Games of Parelli Natural Horse-man-ship*, we are told that these games must be understood before we try to communicate further with the horse. Every single thing that we do with our horses is one or a combination of the Seven Games, says Pat. Each game is numbered, because it is important initially to play them in order while learning and teaching them to the horse. The entire Parelli system is based on these games and developing them to a greater extent, both on the ground and in the saddle, at each level of the program. The first three games are 'principle' games, and Pat likens them to the alphabet on which we build our words and sentences. The last four games are 'purpose' games.

'we need to convince the horse that we are not predators and that we can be trusted'

1 The Friendly Game

The Friendly Game basically involves gently caressing the horse to convince him that you will not act like a predator, and that you are friendly and can be trusted. We are told that we must be able to touch the horse all over. This touching must be in the form of rhythmical rubbing, and not patting. Pat points out that most people pat their horses, but he considers that horses do not like this approach. He also points out that rhythmical rubbing is the first thing a mare will do to her new foal. This 'game' may be of help to new horse owners.

2 The Porcupine Game

The Porcupine Game requires the handler to push the horse gently away physically with the hand, as a reminder that he should not lean against a point of pressure, but should learn to move away from it. This should be done with a steady pressure, starting soft and slowly increasing until the horse responds. Pressure is applied in four phases as required: first the hair, then the skin, then the muscle, and finally the bone. The phases are applied, starting slowly with phase one, until the horse responds. The optimum goal is to be able to use only phase one.

3 The Driving Game

The Driving Game teaches the horse to respond to implied pressure, where you use primarily body language to suggest to the horse to move, and he moves without you touching him. Although initially we may need to be close to the horse, we are told that as we progress through the levels, we can gradually increase the distance.

4 The Yo-Yo Game

The Yo-Yo Game involves sending the horse backwards, mainly from the lead rope being waved up and down, and then bringing him back towards you in a straight line. Backwards and forwards should be equal and light.

As with all the games, Pat stresses that the horse must not be afraid. However, I think that we must be very careful with this game to ensure that our body language does not become aggressive and the game provocative.

5 The Circling Game

The Circling Game is where the handler sends the horse away in a circle around him by means of waving the long line slightly towards the rear of the horse, but Pat is emphatic that this should not be confused with lungeing. There are three parts to the Circling Game he says – the send, the allow and the bring back, all of which need to be done without moving your feet.

With the Circling Game, Pat says that disengagement of the hindquarters (swinging them away from you) is very important, and is how you teach a horse to be easily controlled – mentally, emotionally and physically. It would seem, from my studies of training techniques and questioning of other trainers, that this way of lungeing is the opposite of that advocated by most trainers, where the horse must stop out on the circle. However, Pat does not call it lungeing, and is keen to make a distinction between the two techniques.

'...the horse is instinctively afraid of any small or tight space'

It may seem to viewers of the Parelli video that the horse was 'programmed' to carry on *ad infinitum* until given a further instruction, and, with very little involvement on the part of the trainer, there is perhaps the risk that the horse could get bored and robot-like. However, Pat's own documentation states that horses should do a minimum of two laps and a maximum of four depending on the level and length of line used, and he himself views lungeing as 'mindless'.

6 The Sideways Game

The Sideways Game involves teaching the horse to go sideways equally right and left, with ease.

7 The Squeeze Game

The Squeeze Game appears from the video to be somewhat similar to the Circling Game, except that it involves pushing the horse in between, over and under obstacles. Pat's rationale is that because the horse is instinctively afraid of any small or tight space, the Squeeze Game will teach him to become braver and calmer, and to squeeze through narrow spots – such as loading into a trailer – without concern.

In my opinion, the concept of a horse jumping over obstacles of his own volition is an excellent one, as, for example, with a jumping lane. However, I think we should remember that horses should be given a good approach to a jump, even when not carrying a rider. Also, as Pat points out adamantly in his documentation, you must not allow the horse to receive a yank on the lead rope on landing; you must allow the rope to slide through your hand, and avoid him feeling a jerk backwards on the rope. Viewers may be concerned, from the safety point of view, when the horse on the video was asked to go up a bank, still with the long line attached, and then over a jump with high posts on either side. Pat is extremely adept at throwing the rope over the posts so that the horse does not get caught, but I feel that maybe there should be some word of caution that only experienced horsemen should try this – and preferably under the supervision of experienced Parelli instructors.

Concepts of Partnership – the Parelli Savvy System

This part of the Parelli training programme starts in a very promising manner. Pat Parelli explains how to teach the horse to turn his head towards the handler when the headcollar is put on and off. He does this by using steady pressure of the hand – the Porcupine Game. He goes on to explain how to put on a saddle with consideration for the horse. Although this is very basic, it is sound advice for beginners. He goes on to explain that we should not do up the girth completely straight away, but gently increase the tension a little at a time, after walking the horse around. This is a method that I would like to see used at every equestrian establishment.

Pat proceeds to explain that we should rock the saddle to and fro, in a sideways rocking motion, to prepare the horse for mounting. Viewers of the video must make up their own minds as to the advisability of this procedure. They may like to bear in mind that many trainers advocate the use of a mounting block and/or a person holding the opposite stirrup while mounting. This is to avoid muscular damage, or even spinal pressure, if the saddle is pulled out of place. Of course there are times when mounting with a mounting block or with a person to hold the opposite stirrup is impossible. This is when dexterity of the rider can minimize the discomfort for the horse. I quote from Elwyn Hartley Edwards's book *Saddlery* (JA Allen 1963): 'If one has put the saddle on carefully, it is equally stupid to haul yourself up by cantle and forearch and move it out of place again when mounting. If you have difficulty in mounting easily, use a mounting block or get a leg up.'

After mounting, we are told that the horse should be bent to left and right. This involves lateral flexion by the rider leading the horse's head around to the rider's leg. This kind of flexion may be fine if the horse were doing it on his own, say to accept a sugar lump, but the fact that the horse is being pulled gives him no choice in the matter. Perhaps we should look to the classical masters again for their advice on this matter. Here is what Waldemar Seunig writes in his book *Horsemanship*: 'The unsteady or sawing hand which pulls the neck to the right and to the left from its base (the part that should be steadiest), weakens the scalenus muscle, interfering with it to such an extent that it grows limp and is unable to do one of its jobs, holding the ribs and sternum up to the front.' Seunig writes further on this, again in *Horsemanship*: 'The horse's neck must arise from a firm broad foundation, like a fishing rod, whose lower end is almost unbending, but whose upper (towards the poll) end must be thin, elastic and flexible.'

'we should not do up the girth completely straight away, but gently increase the tension a little at a time'

General Decarpentry writes in *Academic Equitation*: 'The moment the horse is bent to his limit, he finds that he is obliged to straighten himself out again. If he cannot straighten his neck which the hand forces to remain bent, he throws his quarters out in the opposite direction to escape the bend.'

All the classical masters, past and present, taught that the flexibility of the spine must be continuous through the entire body of the horse, and never limited to one specific spot, particularly not the withers, which will disconnect the horse and place him on the forehand. Obviously, this is another point on which viewers of Pat's video and my readers must make up their own minds.

The riding seems to be mostly done in a type of rope pressure-halter. Pat Parelli calls this a hackamore. He has a lead rope attached to the underneath of this halter. The lead rope is thrown over the horse's head each time a change of direction is required, using a stick (carrot stick) to push the horse around on the opposite side. To 'ask' for a halt, Pat Parelli advocates again leading the horse's head around towards the rider's leg. The horse has little choice but to stop.

Summary and Conclusions

Pat points out that we want to be the horse's friend and we want him as our 'partner'. However, this does seem to be slightly contradicted when he tells us that we must become the horse's alpha and makes statements such as 'we need to programme the horse to do what we want him to do' and 'we must win the games'.

Pat talks about four phases of firmness, which can range from gentle into discomfort. The horse's reward, when doing what the trainer requires, is that the discomfort is ceased or diminished. While clearly the rider/trainer needs to be in control of the horse, and the horse must be obedient, it should, in my opinion, be possible for the trainer to make it easy for the horse to obey. In other words, we should not ask the horse to do anything for which he has not been well prepared. We should make sure that he is well able to perform the desired movement, as well as to be sure that he understands what is required of him. In the event of

'we should not ask the horse to do anything for which he has not been well prepared'

it becoming evident that either of the above criteria has not been fulfilled, then the trainer should recognise this and cease the exercise.

Pat Parelli does point out, many times on the audio as well as on the video tapes, the excellent idea of acquiring fingers and legs that close slowly and open quickly. He was applying this principle to the lead rope when asking the horse to move forward. As soon as the horse gives a little, then the fingers open. He also applied this principle to ridden work with the legs and hand. This is a very good explanation of how to learn to 'give' the rein when riding, in other words when the horse 'gives'.

During the Circling Game, when the horse is sent on a very small circle, it could have been helpful to mention the fact that lungeing, or circling, is extremely tiring, particularly for a young or elderly horse. Although some of Pat's documentation states clearly that the number of circles should be limited, a warning on the video might have been useful in preventing possible misuse of the game. Lungeing is considered by most trainers to be invaluable when done correctly, ie gently and only for short spells initially on a large circle, building up to smaller circles when the horse has built up its stamina, balance, and is sufficiently strong and supple. The smaller the circle, the harder it is for the horse, and the more stress is put upon joints, tendons and ligaments. When carried out indiscriminately and without gentle preparation, lungeing can cause strain and mental stress. I am sure that this is not Pat's intention in any way with the Circling Game, but nevertheless I feel that his instructions and warnings should be more comprehensive, as people may be using the game without the training or supervision of Parelli instructors.

During the Sideways Game, the horse is pushed sideways, and there is the potential (although not the intention) for this to be done in an abrupt and repetitive manner. It may have been helpful at this point to mention that these lateral (sideways) movements are strenuous when first attempted by the horse. The first lateral steps should be approached gently, slowly, and tactfully. One or two steps should suffice for the first attempt, and the degree of lateral bend and cross-over of legs can be slowly built up, as the horse's joints strengthen and become more supple.

Here is what Col. Podhajsky has to say, again from *The Complete Training of Horse and Rider* about training lateral movements: 'The term 'lateral work' includes all those movements in which the horse *not only steps forward but sideways* (my emphasis). These movements are not performed by young horses at liberty and should be taught only after appropriate progress has been made in the physical training of the horse'.

> '...lateral movements are strenuous when first attempted by the horse'

Many people may well consider that the horses trained by the Parelli Natural Horsemanship method are actually very well 'programmed' as they perform all the exercises and 'tricks', such as standing on logs or spinning round. However, on the video they may appear to be lacking in self-expression – although clearly from Pat's own documentation, this is not what he intends.

I feel sure that Pat Parelli has devised his method of training with the best interests of the horses at heart, but is it possible that he has gone a step too far in his attempt to be the 'alpha horse' or 'head of the herd'?

An exception to the above 'switched-off' look was the exact opposite which I encountered at the Equus Event in 2002. To my delight, in came a lady called Silke Vallentin with a black Friesian horse called Biko. This was a large heavy horse with lovely feathers down his legs. Silke was in an electric vehicle, which I have since learned she prefers to think of as a motor bike! She certainly handled it as if it were a very agile motor bike. Silke and Biko played around the arena, with Biko showing beautiful, free paces, full of expression and in self-carriage. Biko would 'dance' around Silke as the 'motor bike' spun around. It was such a wonderful sight, the crowd went wild.

There were many comments at the end of that day to the effect that Silke and Biko gave the best performance of the entire day. Silke's motor bike was adapted in such a way as to accommodate the carriage of various whips with which she could indicate and direct Biko's movements.

Silke is a 3* Parelli Instructor and demonstrates Pat Parelli's methods at clinics in her home country of Germany and is frequently in the UK giving demonstrations and teaching as a visiting instructor. Silke told me: 'Before discovering Parelli Natural Horsemanship, I did try some other methods, but without success and therefore experienced some very dangerous situations.' Presumably Silke's training had been the same as the other Parelli students, but somehow the horse has perceived the whole picture in a different manner. Biko was by far the largest of any of the Parelli students'

horses I have ever seen (including live performances and videos), and it occurs to me that this might have had an impact on the way in which Silke had carried out the Parelli training. In addition, Silke being on a 'motor bike' may have had an effect. I should imagine that Silke would not have dominated her horse or used such aggressive body language as a person standing upright. My guess is that she used a much more subtle approach, but whatever the case, it certainly worked and gave me much food for thought.

While, in principle, it is clear that we must take the lead in our partnership with our horses, surely it is possible to do this without undermining the horses' input? I am sure that horses have a need for self-esteem. If their training system does not allow for the occasional error or misunderstanding, then the horse will resort to behaving more like a robot than a living creature, for fear of a rebuke. One of the main rebukes in this training method seems to be repeated abrupt stops. The line between too much discipline and too little has to be drawn in different places for different horses,

'Biko would 'dance' around Silke as the motor bike spun around'

as their temperaments and needs may vary greatly. While the Parelli system certainly does not deliberately employ physically cruel methods, it may be that it does little for a horse's self-esteem, and relies too heavily on the trainer becoming similar to the matriarchal mare in the wild-herd situation. What may be forgotten here is the fact that this mare may never actually be 'friends' with her subordinates, and friendship with our horses is what Parelli, and most of us, are aiming for.

An experienced horseman, such as Pat Parelli, has a wonderful feel for what is correct for a particular horse at a given moment in time. There is perhaps a danger, when people depart from the established principles of horsemanship, that they may not interpret or apply the new principles correctly, and the results could be totally different from what is intended.

Many of Pat Parelli's philosophies are excellent, and I know of many brilliant trainers who have incorporated Parelli methods into their training programmes with great success.

> '... and friendship with our horses is what Parelli,
> and most of us, are aiming for'

CHAPTER 7

Monty Roberts

Understanding the Body Language of Horses

'I have not created anything. I have not invented
anything. I have only discovered what nature
already had in place'

Monty Roberts introduced one of the first 'alternative' training methods to receive public acclaim in the UK. Not only has he received public recognition, but he has received the royal seal of approval. In April 1989, Her Majesty the Queen requested that he should visit her and give a private demonstration at Windsor Castle; his work with the virtually untouched youngsters was an outstanding success. Her Majesty the Queen Mother was reportedly moved to tears when a frightened young filly was transformed into an animal with quiet confidence who stood steady as a rock, with no head restraint, while a saddle was put on her back. After just 25 minutes, she had accepted both the bridle and a rider.

The Queen's interest in this method of dealing with young and/or difficult horses may well have been prompted by some of the problems encountered with her racehorses; she was undoubtedly very impressed. I understand from a spokesman for the King's Troop, that Monty's methods were introduced following his visit and are still sometimes used to start young horses today, depending on how the horse reacts. I am told that all recruits to the main King's Troop and Household Cavalry training centre at Melton Mowbray in Leicestershire receive thorough training in conventional British 'backing' methods, as well as a knowledge of Monty Roberts' methods. It would seem that they are endeavouring to utilize the best of each method to suit the individual horse.

'it is never easy to go against convention; it takes a special kind of person…'

My guess is that when Monty Roberts first visited the royal stables, his methods may have upset a number of the exponents of the 'old school of training'. Considering that, up until then, they had been reasonably successfully undertaking the job in hand, this scepticism would be understandable to a certain extent. In some cases, they may have had a lifetime of loyal service behind them – and who could blame them for feeling suspicious of an unknown American with some very unusual ideas?

In his book *The Man Who Listens to Horses* (Random House Press 1986), Monty hinted at this slight atmosphere of animosity. On a few occasions, he was presented with situations that were less than ideal and somewhat unfair, not to mention dangerous. For instance, two three-year-old piebald stallions were presented to him for join-up. They had hardly been handled, and had spent all their lives together in a field at Hampton Court. Monty was not given an opportunity before the demonstration to acclimatize these horses to the round pen – something he normally does – and as soon as one horse was taken away from the other, they both started screaming frantically. This would seem to me to be testing his abilities unnecessarily to the limit and was hardly fair on the horses. Nevertheless, Monty did manage to 'join-up' with both these stallions very successfully, but it must have been extremely nerve racking, especially in the presence of the Queen.

I take my hat off to Monty Roberts for continuing with his kinder way of starting a young horse when, prior to this royal interest, many people were against him. It is never easy to go against convention, and it takes a special kind of person to shrug off the inevitable ridicule and jibes. The kindness in his heart towards the equine species, and his conviction in the validity of his methods, are self-evident. His subsequent success and fame are thus, in my opinion, very well earned.

I believe that his methods are far preferable to the rough and non-caring treatment that many horses experience. However, the classical way of backing a young horse is also without pain or stress to the horse although it takes considerably longer.

'…these ideas suggest that horses think in the same egocentric way that we do'

I fully agree with Monty's general ethos of making the horse 'want' to be with him and to work for him. I quote now from Kelly Marks, one of his British protégés:

'I believe one of the most common reasons for treating horses over-harshly is human conceit. Thoughts like 'I'd never let a horse make a fool of me' or 'I've started doing it this way, so I can't back down or he'll know he's won' are ideas that suggest that horses think in the same egocentric way that we do.' (Kelly Marks *Intelligent Horsemanship* leaflet).

Kelly's statement echoes the classical ethos of humility and open-mindedness, and I endorse it wholeheartedly.

What we should examine is Monty's statement that we should make it comfortable for the horse when he is doing what we want and uncomfortable for him when he is doing what we do *not* want. The first part of this statement is fine, but what about making it 'uncomfortable' – do we really *need* to do this? Although, in most situations, I do not like to see a horse subjected to any discomfort, I recognise that in some instances, as the lesser of two evils, it could be in the horse's best interests in the long run.

Although I appreciate that no horse fully loses its 'flight' instinct, it is important to recognise the subtle differences when dealing with horses who have been well domesticated for centuries, as compared with recently tamed mustangs. This is a point that occurs to me repeatedly when reviewing Monty's methods of training. All horses do share the 'flight' instinct, but they do not all respond in exactly the same way in their training. Not only can the 'flight' instinct be overcome to a considerable extent through training (as with police horses, for example), but for some horses it has become 'watered down' simply through generations of horses being kept in relatively small fields with no predators to worry about.

Obviously, after this royal interest, increasing numbers of eminent horse people, as well as everyday riders, became interested in what was seen to be a revolutionary way of training horses. As a spin-off from Monty's popularity in the UK, he has trained several pupils who are now practising his methods and training others. Kelly Marks, perhaps his most well-known protégée, runs courses in Monty Roberts Horsemanship, entitled *Intelligent Horsemanship* in Oxfordshire, UK. As one would expect, she has personalized this system, adding some of her own ideas, but without deviating from Monty's basic teaching (see Chapter 3). Kelly is also a regular writer in popular equestrian magazines, as well as having taken part in a television series called *Barking Mad*. Other Monty Roberts instructors have also become very popular, writing articles in magazines, doing lecture/demo tours, and also appearing on television.

It would seem that we, the public, are not just mildly interested in these alternative methods – even non-horsey members of the public are hungry to learn more about it. Could it be that there is an element of magical fascination here? To people who know nothing at all about horses, some of Monty Roberts' methods must seem to be almost magical. To others who have been around horses all their lives, their behavioural reactions may not seem so surprising.

Here we will take a closer look at these methods in an attempt to understand and assess the desirability of using them in the day-to-day training of the average riding horse.

The Join-Up Technique

I first saw Monty Roberts perform his join-up technique during one of his demonstration tours in the early 1990s, knowing little or nothing about his methods and, therefore, with no pre-conceived ideas. I have recently attended more of his demonstrations, during which the process of join-up was carried out in exactly the same way as all those years ago (it has obviously stood the test of time). I am absolutely convinced that he has managed to understand the body language of horses and is able to communicate with them in their own language, using body posture, which the horses obviously understand. This is certainly a remarkable achievement which, to my knowledge, has never been presented in this way before.

His join-up technique is based on his theory of 'advance-and-retreat'. He observed this phenomenon when, as a boy in Nevada, he was in the process of rounding up and catching a herd of wild mustangs. He found that when he followed them for a number of miles, and then turned back the opposite way, the horses would turn to follow him. This was obviously instinctive behaviour and happened time and time again, and he used it to help him manoeuvre the horses to where a corral had been set up for them.

Monty also observed a matriarchal mare (the leader of the herd is usually a mare, not a stallion, as many people believe) disciplining a disruptive young colt, after the colt had been too aggressive in its play and was annoying some of the mares. The matriarch singled out this colt and drove it well away from the herd – quite the worst place for a wild horse to be, as a single animal out on its own is more likely to be picked on by a predator. It was not until the colt showed signs of submissive behaviour that he was allowed back into the herd. It is this submissive behaviour, such as chewing or lowering the head, that Monty looks for in his join-up technique, before he invites the horse back towards him (as described below). After the colt had been allowed back into the herd, he behaved well for a while, but then started his disruptive antics again, whereupon he was driven away another time by the mare. Eventually, the colt understood that he must behave in order to be allowed to live in the herd. Monty's body language is directly modelled on the body posture of the matriarchal mare disciplining the colt.

For his join-up, Monty uses a round pen, which is usually a metal enclosure of about 50 feet (15m) in diameter. First, he sends the horse around the pen by standing a little behind him, although out of kicking reach, and, using aggressive body language, with arms raised and eyes fixed directly on the horse, he flings a long line at the horse's quarters. With young, unbroken and often unhandled horses, this sends them around the pen quite fast. The line is pitched at the horse to keep him going each time he looks as though he is tiring or relaxing. The aggressive body language is continued with Monty making his shoulder axis square with the horse's head. 'Blocking' his path in aggressive mode, and again using the long line, Monty changes the direction of movement of the horse around the pen.

'Monty's body posture is that of the matriarchial mare disciplining the colt'

We are told that the natural flight distance of the horse in the wild is a quarter of a mile, and after the horse has been around the pen five or six times in each direction, that will be approximately the distance he has covered. Monty then expects to see the horse giving body signals that he is ready to give up his flight and give respect to his human 'chaser', and would like to come in closer and be more comfortable. He calls this the language of 'Equus'. The head of the horse usually begins to tip, and the neck bends slightly to bring the head closer to the inside of the circle. The inside ear will be moving towards Monty, and usually his head will be lowered. Another sign of 'submission' is a chewing and licking movement in his mouth.

At this point, Monty loses his aggressive stance and assumes a submissive mode. He turns away from the horse with eyes down and shoulders slightly hunched. The long line is then coiled up. If the horse does not follow at this point, he is put back to flight for a few more laps. Each horse I saw was soon following Monty around the pen as a foal would follow its mother. After this 'leading-without-a-lead-rein' procedure, Monty then starts to touch the horse. He has an artificial arm, which he uses as an extension to his arm, to reach some of the vulnerable and tricky areas, ie the places on the horse's body where a predator would first attack. When he has successfully touched all over the horse, including down each leg, with no head control on the horse, Monty then calls for a saddle to be brought out, which is initially laid on the ground, and the horse is allowed to look at it and smell it. The saddle is then very gently and carefully put on the horse's back, and the girth is done up slowly. The horse is still not restrained by the head in any way.

The first thing that struck me was that the horse looked frightened when sent away by the long line being thrown towards him. (The line never actually touches the horse.) The horse obviously had no idea why the line was being aimed at him, and it was quite natural for him to want to flee from it. Everything that Monty did, explaining his body language as he did it, was reflected in the horse exactly as he predicted. Monty obviously knew the way the horse would think and react. However, I pose the question: do we want initially to frighten our horses so that they will only want to be with us because it is the line of least resistance (the lesser of the two evils)? Or do we want them to actually 'want' to be with us? Nevertheless, the horse looked anything but frightened after the join-up procedure.

'within 30 minutes, the reluctant loader was walking in and out of the trailer…'

During his demonstrations, after the initial sending away in the join-up procedure, Monty talks to the horse very gently. Well, actually, he is talking to the audience, explaining what the horse is saying and thinking, in a very entertaining, enjoyable way. I am sure that his gentle, soothing voice was just as enjoyable to the horse and went a huge way towards keeping the horse calm and his adrenaline levels low.

When Monty was working with an older horse with a behavioural problem – in this case loading into a trailer – Monty's first task was to join-up with him. This was shown to be much more difficult with the horse that has already received training and is used to being handled, and no doubt used to having relationships with humans. My feeling was that it was even more stressful to be chased away with the long line. It certainly took a lot more waving and aggressive body language from Monty to instigate the fleeing reaction. My heart went out to this horse, as it must have wondered what on earth was going on – why was it being chased away in this aggressive manner? In my opinion, this cannot be likened to lungeing or loose schooling, where the horse is gently encouraged to move by the handler's voice and guiding whip. When used correctly as an extension to the human arm, the whip can be a real comfort to the horse in giving him his parameters within which to work.

Nevertheless, within about 30 minutes of achieving join-up, the reluctant loader was walking in and out of the trailer, with Monty holding a completely loose lead rein. Eventually, the horse would walk in and out of the trailer very happily, with no lead line, and at one point did so completely alone without human intervention. Once again, I had every admiration for Monty's achievement. His way of winning the horse's confidence and getting him to do what was required may not have been completely stress-free in the first instance, but it was certainly much better than what often happens to horses that refuse to load! We have all seen the shouting, tugging, whipping and so on.

On the other hand, parking the trailer in the horse's field and feeding him, first on the ramp, and gradually further up, until finally inside, would probably have worked just as well – depending, of course, on what had caused the horse's fear or dislike of the trailer in the first place. This more conventional approach would undoubtedly have taken much longer, however.

At the first demonstration that I attended by Monty back in the 1990s, he was advocating, and indeed using in the demonstration, his own 'Be Nice' halter. This is a relatively narrow rope halter, designed in such a way that if the horse should resist or try to pull away, pressure is applied automatically over the poll, on the nose, and behind the horse's jaw. This halter has blunt pressure studs over the poll area that can be applied or not, depending on how the halter is fitted. Purchasers are told that a horse should never be tied up in a 'Be Nice' halter, that it is for training only, and that the pressure is released instantly as soon as the horse moves in the required direction.

This halter could be a very useful training device in the right hands, but in the wrong hands, in my opinion, it could be quite damaging. Stallion chains have been used traditionally for a similar purpose as the 'Be Nice' halter. Many people think that stallion chains are cruel, but here again they can be useful in the right hands, and in my opinion are necessary in some instances. I would rather see a horse controlled in this way than have the animal escape and gallop onto a road. I think that the use of the 'Be Nice' halter should be confined to experienced horse people, as is Monty's intention.

At the recent demonstration that I attended, Monty was using, and advocating, his later invention called the Dually halter (pronounced 'Dooley'). This is a milder controller halter than the 'Be Nice', and Monty recommends it for more sensitive horses, for young horses, and for less experienced handlers. It seems to have largely overtaken the 'Be Nice', although both are still on the market. It has a dual purpose in that it has two rings; one can be used for training and one to tie up. The training part of the halter consists of a double rope across the horse's nose, which passes through rings on either side of the head. If the horse pulls, pressure will be exerted on the nose. This pressure should be released when the horse stops pulling. Obviously, this pressure will also be exerted if the handler pulls. Therefore, like most tools, it is open to abuse. However, I understand that a video is available showing the correct and proper use of this halter.

'I would rather see a horse controlled in this way than have the animal escape and gallop onto a road'

The Dually has two additional rings, either side of the horse's head, at the ends of the double rope that sits over the nose, to which reins can be attached so that the halter can then be used for riding purposes. In fact, during the Kelly Marks demonstration that I saw, Kelly was riding and jumping her horse in the Dually.

Monty also markets something he calls a 'Wip Wop Rope', which is a short, soft rope with a tasselled end. It sends visual and auditory cues to the horse to encourage forward movement and doesn't come into contact with the horse's body. This is obviously because he is so against the use of whips, but I am sure that if someone wanted to inflict pain, it could be done with a rope. It is interesting to note that he feels the need for something to use as an 'extension-to-the-arm' aid. Nevertheless, the intention is good.

QUESTION 1: *I know you have said that you are against lungeing with one lunge line, but do you think that there are exceptions to this, eg when lungeing is done properly?*

MONTY'S REPLY: There is no proper single-line lungeing at all. Single-line lungeing is the second worst piece of horsemanship on earth. Single-line lungeing with fixed side-reins with elastic in them is better than classical lungeing with a noseband with steel in it and a ring on the top of the nose, which is probably the second worst thing that a person can do with a horse, because it puts the body totally in the wrong position. It puts the spine in the wrong position, it puts the neck in the wrong position, it puts the leading legs in the wrong position, and it does just about everything that is wrong to do with a horse. If you single-line lunge a horse for about 30 days when it is a yearling or two years of age, and never did it again, when that horse is about fifteen years old, I would be able to tell you that it had been single-line lunged – an awful piece of horsemanship!

QUESTION 2: *You say in your book that horses are 'into-pressure' animals. Do you mean that they push back towards a steady pressure, and not to a nudge? I refer to a mare with her foal nudging it away. Could you elaborate on this subject please?*

MONTY'S REPLY: Horses are 'into-pressure' animals with relation to any pressure that you put on them, whether steady or intermittent. When a mare nudges a foal away, the foal will try to nudge back into the mother. When you lay your left leg on they will move left, when you lay your right leg on them they will move right. This is because when a big cat attacks them, it is a very effective way for them to survive, to move towards the cat rather than away. That way there will be less flesh torn. Because we are so 'off pressure', it is better, when we ride them, for us to train them to do it our way. I like to go with the horse's natural tendencies as much as possible, but to train a horse to move away from pressure is probably a wise thing to do.

QUESTION 3: *Do you think that it is fair, or kind, for racehorses to be expected to race at the age of two, when they are still virtually 'babies', and their limbs and growth plates are not properly formed?*

MONTY'S REPLY: Horses mature at a rate, so that now it is quantified by the epiphyseal closures at the ends of the long bones. I do not believe in racing horses, or doing much else with horses, until they will X-ray 'A' in their epiphyseal closures. 'A' means that they are fully mature, that it is bone and no longer the growth-plate cartilage that you find at the epiphyseal closures of the long bones.

For people to take the position that two-year-olds should not be raced is incredibly inept. If you look at the racing industry and say that we should ban two-year-old racing, you have to also say then what would happen. In my opinion, it would be one of the most cruel things that you could ever do, to completely ban two-year-old racing. If you did, and you remained the same otherwise, then you would see such a cavalry charge after 1st January of horses in their third year. People would be trying to get their horses to every

'the closer horses are to their human owners, the more they need join-up, and the more my techniques will work'

Derby all around the world. Horses would be run off their legs at an early age, maybe when they were not even mature enough to do it. If you did not race two-year-olds, then you would have to sell two-year-olds instead of yearlings, and then the colts would have to be separated. All the stud farms would have to have separate pastures for their Thoroughbred colts, because Thoroughbreds would destroy themselves left out in bands of full-on colts in their two-year-old year, particularly if you fed them enough to realise a high enough price in a 'baby' sale. The desperate things that would happen if two-year-old racing were banned would outweigh the problems caused by two-year-old racing a hundred times.

Do I believe in two-year-old racing? – no. Do I believe in racing horses who X-ray less than 'A' in their epiphyseal closures? – no. However, you have to be responsible when you make decisions, so you have to look at both sides of each of the subjects and ask 'what would happen if this was done?', and in the case of banning two-year-old racing, it would be disastrous.

QUESTION 4: *Do you think that there are horses who are already very close to their human owners (and therefore understand the human language) and for whom your join-up technique would be impossible, or perhaps pointless?*

MONTY'S REPLY: The closer horses are to their human owners, the more they need join-up, and the more my techniques will work. Horses who are bonded to the human and over-humanized, in many instances, need join-up desperately. They need to know how to be a horse and how to respond naturally to people. So many people think 'My horse loves me and he stays near me, I don't need to do join-up'. That is the person who needs to do it most. Horses become so rude and overwhelming in their lack of ground manners when they are overly bonded with people without join-up. Horses need to go away and learn to come back, and the communication system will not kick in properly until you can go both ways. Every single mare on the face of the earth, knows this – why we human beings cannot figure this out is far more than I will ever know.

QUESTION 5: *Do you find a great difference in the understanding of Equus between a horse whose ancestry is domesticated compared with, say, a wild Mustang? Has the domesticated horse become de-sensitized to its own language?*

MONTY'S REPLY: Often times, the domesticated horse has become de-sensitized to its own language and too humanized. This question is closely related to the previous question. To over-humanize does mask over their own language; there is no question about that. How to prove this is to take orphan foals, raise them with humans instead of horses and see what happens. Observe their behavioural patterns when they are growing up and when they are adults. You will find that they have to see and learn their language. Very little of this process is instinctive.

I had the opportunity recently to start a horse that was born deaf. He had had the opportunity to see his mother and other horses, but had never heard a sound in his life. He had been scientifically proven to be profoundly deaf, but that horse understood his own language perfectly. In the same year, I had on offer to me a horse that had been born blind and then at two years of age had surgery to remove two huge cataracts over the eyes – the horse could then see, and he knew absolutely nothing about his language because he couldn't see the body language of the other horses. Therein lies the proof that horses must be allowed to learn their language and be taught the language by other horses. Orphans prove it to you, and blind and deaf horses prove it too.

If you just take domestication as a criterion and you utilize domestication with undomesticated horses, you will find a significant difference in how they respond, but I find that the significant difference is greater as the predators are larger and more predominant. In Australia, for instance, there are very few predators. There are a few dingos, but to the Brumby there is no mountain lion, no wolf pack, no grizzly bears – no large predators that harvest the Brumby. The brumby will respond to people slightly differently from the American Mustang, who is subject to large predators that take them up to, say, one year of age; their upbringing is significantly different. I think it is basically established through their experience with a predator and not because of historical domestication.

You can take historically domesticated horses and turn them out in the wild with mustangs and if they live, and only a small percentage of them will live, then within about 18 months they will respond as a wild mustang. They return to the wild in every way. When you turn out a young Thoroughbred into the wild, if he lives, within 18 months, the walls of his feet will be three times thicker than when he was turned out. The same sort of thing happens to deer when returned to the wild, as well as pigs, whose skin will become three times thicker in a similar period of time. The 300 per cent increase seems to happen time and time again. This seems to be the difference between domestication and living in the wild.

'I don't believe whipping a horse is ever appropriate – before Pat Parelli dies, he will agree with me'

QUESTION 6: *What do you think of Parelli Natural Horsemanship?*

MONTY'S REPLY: I am a fan and a supporter of anybody who advocates the training of horses with the lack of pain, restraint, pressure and violence. Parelli does some things that I do not agree with, but on balance he does a lot of good things and he helps a lot of people with their horses, and I agree with a lot of things he does. Parelli has spent time with me, spent some time on my farm, and I have had him do demonstrations and clinics at my farm. I have known him since he was a little boy and he is a good guy and does, in my opinion, good work. However, he does some things that are not acceptable to me, and one is the use of a whip. I don't believe that whipping a horse is ever appropriate. That is my position – before Pat Parelli dies, he will agree with me. He is thinking it over now.

A whip drives adrenaline up; that's all a whip can do – it is never an instrument you can use to bring adrenaline down. Horses do not learn when adrenaline is up; they learn when it is down. Whips should be banned, they should be burned up, and anyone who whips on a horse to cause pain should be arrested. Whips can be used to communicate, as in dressage. If they are not used for pain, I have no problem with them – that is my position. However, Pat Parelli does a lot of good work, and I do not want to be negative about him.

QUESTION 7: *Have you ever studied the works of the great classical riding masters, and, if so, do you think that your methods are vastly different, or that the two can be combined and perhaps overlap?*

MONTY'S REPLY: I have studied a lot of the classical masters. I could take you, even today, to see places on the European continent where descendants of the masters are training in the classical way, and their training is overtly brutal. They are felons in my opinion; they should be arrested and prosecuted for brutality. I am certainly not saying that all the masters were bad horsemen; they were not – there was some wonderful horsemanship amongst them. I am thinking of people such as Jimmy Williams who studied the masters and showed dressage horses and jumping horses, gaited horses and fine harness horses, as well as cutting horses and rein cow horses. As he grew older (he died in his eighties) he became less and less brutal, but he was trained in some of the early classical ways. That is not to paint all classical riders with the brush of brutality. There are many things about classical riding that are incredibly good.

'you have to study my methods in detail to decipher these things'

QUESTION 8: *Do you think that the ethos of Sylvia Loch and the Classical Riding Club and your methods are basically working along the same lines?*

MONTY'S REPLY: I think that Sylvia Loch's training techniques have a whole lot of similarities to my work. Many dressage riders, including some of the American dressage riders who have competed at Olympic level – including Charlotte Bradall (a bronze medal winner in Spain) and Camilla DuPont – have taken up my methods and would not vary so much from Sylvia Loch.

You have to study my methods in detail to decipher these things. My methods are to allow the horse to do anything that it wants to do, and then be uncomfortable when it does the negative thing and comfortable when it does what you perceive to be the positive thing. That is all it is – those are my methods, they are based upon the language of the horse, which I can demonstrate to anyone, is a sound, scientific and actual language that is predictable, discernible and effective. That's what it takes to make a language, and that's what the language is. I can predict it, and you can see it, and it is effective. It is effective to the extent that I have absolutely turned the world around in its position as to how long it takes a horse to accept its first saddle, bridle and rider. That is just one thing that my concepts speak of, but it is true that nobody before me ever said that it took less than four to six weeks for a horse to accept its first saddle, bridle and rider. This is not because the horses have changed – horses are exactly the same – but because we have changed our approach to working with horses.

QUESTION 9: *Are there any horses with whom you would never use join-up?*

MONTY'S REPLY: To ask this question, you would have to fail utterly to understand what join-up is. Join-up is the horses' language; they use it all the time with one another, and they use it with other animals too – if other animals would bother to observe what they are doing and respond to their language. This question is like asking 'Are there any Americans that you would refuse to speak English with?' – no. The horses use join-up, I don't; I have only bought into what they already have as a language.

'the language of the horse is a sound, scientific
and actual language that is predictable,
discernible and effective'

Summary and Conclusions

Unfortunately, I did not have time to engage Monty in in-depth discussions regarding his replies to my questions. His replies were very detailed and concise, and I am grateful to him for the time he took to answer in an otherwise hectic schedule.

Lungeing

Monty clearly has very strong views on lungeing and is totally against lungeing with a single line. I have never, myself, seen a horse that has been damaged by correct lungeing, but many people do not lunge correctly. It may be the potential of lungeing to be misused that has caused Monty to come to such a strong position; he has perhaps witnessed some very harsh lungeing that has been carried out for too long, too soon in the horse's career. Correct lungeing requires a gradual introduction to this exercise, being careful not to over-lunge at too early an age.

The age at which one can start lungeing must depend on the individual horse. Some horses, particularly big horses, are not sufficiently balanced or mature enough to canter on the lunge until they are at least five years of age. I would go so far as to say that some young large horses should not canter in a small circle, such as the round pen, until they are gently prepared in walk and trot, over a number of weeks or months. That is not to say that they cannot be lunged gently in walk and trot and taught the rudiments of the aids, while, at the same time, this work will help them to learn to balance and will strengthen their joints. When introduced into the horse's curriculum correctly, lungeing will help build up the horse's muscles in preparation for carrying the rider. Obviously, the larger the horse, the more strenuous any work on a small circle will be. However, the size of the circle during lunge work can be increased for larger horses by the trainer walking a circle. As the horse grows stronger and more balanced, the circle can then be gradually decreased in size over the weeks.

'lungeing will help build up the horse's muscles in preparation for the rider'

The problem is – and I think this may be what has influenced Monty's views – that many horses are over-lunged at too early an age, on too small a circle. To make matters even worse, many people never let out the rein to its full length, and when asked why, they cannot usually answer. When the dangers are pointed out, they often still do not let the rein out!

I concur with Monty's view that lungeing with side-reins is better than lungeing without side-reins for many horses. Correctly adjusted side-reins are a benefit to any horse that may have suffered a front-leg injury, such as tendon or joint problems, as they can help the horse to work in a better outline, thus not placing too much weight on the forehand. I would stress here that the length adjustment of the side-reins is crucial. They must not be so short as to pull the horse's head inwards, but just short enough to give the horse a guideline within which to work. Unfortunately, there is no hard and fast rule as to how long the 'correct adjustment' should be. It differs with every horse, not only because of neck length, but also with the stage of training of the horse.

'the horse seems to understand by magic the request of the handler on the ground'

A horse with well developed top-line muscles, who has been trained and is therefore able to carry more weight on his quarters, will need to have the side-reins shorter than the young horse, who is naturally more on the forehand. Many trainers believe that it is good to lunge a horse sometimes without side-reins, so as to enable him to stretch down, relax and become more supple. I am sure that this is the case with some horses, but I feel that we should bear in mind the question of weight on the forehand, and each horse must be treated as an individual. If in doubt I would always ask for advice from a professional equine therapist.

Although Monty Roberts is so vehemently against lungeing with a single line, he does advocate lungeing with two lunge lines, similar to long-reining on a circle – I've seen him do it. This type of long-reining has been used extensively by classical trainers for centuries. There are slight variations in the way that the reins are attached, but all the traditional methods share basically the same objective. This is normally that the trainer does not have to keep the horse on a circle, but can take the horse down the long side of an arena, and even perform lateral work, when horse and trainer are sufficiently proficient. The trainer walks or sometimes runs, either behind or alongside the horse, and uses the reins in a similar way as when mounted. There are usually some magnificent displays of this work at the Spanish Riding School performances, where the horse seems to understand by magic the requests of the handler on the ground. The horse will glide sideways into the most expressive, beautiful half-pass, and the aids are given in such a discreet, gentle way, that they seem indiscernible to the onlooker. However, most classical trainers (including the Spanish Riding School) do employ single-line lungeing at the start of all basic training, as well as using this method to teach a deep, independent seat to the rider.

During traditional training, long-reining is also often carried out on a circle. In this instance, it is very similar to Monty's long-lining in the round pen.

Horses As 'Into-Pressure' Animals

Monty's premiss that horses are 'into-pressure' animals is an intriguing one. His assertion is that if you put a finger of pressure, say, onto a horse's shoulder, he will move towards that pressure. I have always found exactly the opposite, but maybe that is because, when domesticated, horses learn very quickly to move away from pressure;

and being eager to please, this soon becomes a habit. I have seen mares with foals moving their offspring around by gentle pushes, and I cannot say that I have ever seen a foal push back – but that is not to say that it never happens. I understand from Monty's book *The Man Who Listens to Horses* that his belief that horses are 'into-pressure' animals comes from the fact that in a wild situation, when attacked by a big cat, the horse will actually move into the predator's bite, as moving away from it would mean that more flesh would be ripped open. Such a move towards pressure may well be so in this instance, but I would like to see more evidence that this instinct is carried through the horse's entire life.

'I must stress that this pressure need only be extremely light and not visible to the onlooker'

The issue of horses being 'into-pressure' animals may be one that is worth further consideration. Many conventional trainers believe that horses push against sustained pressure and move away from intermittent pressure. Perhaps the amount of pressure sometimes dictates whether they move towards or away from it? However, whatever their natural instincts in this respect may be, it is obvious that it is relatively easy to train a horse to move away from a slight pressure. My experience has always been that most horses that have been trained to the appropriate level, when riding lateral dressage movements, will continue to move away from my leg if a very light pressure is maintained. The sideways movement is then ceased when the leg is relaxed. I must stress that this pressure need only be extremely light and not visible to the onlooker, just a tension of the leg muscles. However, a number of eminent trainers do advocate a series of gentle taps as being preferable to a sustained push.

Two-Year-Old Racing

Monty's answer to my question concerning whether it is fair, or kind, for racehorses to be expected to race at the age of two, was most illuminating and seems very sound common sense.

The Equus Language and the Domesticated Horse

I have combined my comments on Monty's answers to questions 4 and 5 as they are so closely related. Monty's answers are fascinating, and I accept most of what he says. However, I differ in certain respects, in that I feel that there are some very sensitive and well-bonded horses who may be quite frightened by the initial join-up technique. They have come to view humans in a totally different light and understand the human language (verbal and otherwise) sometimes better than we understand it ourselves. We should be cautious when using the Equus language with some horses. In addition, it may be possible that some people are not suited to using this technique. If it is not done with care, like most things, there is the potential for considerable damage.

Monty's observations and theories regarding the responses of horses in relation to the predators that they have encountered seem quite logical and are interesting.

Parelli Natural Horsemanship

Monty's opinions on Parelli Natural Horsemanship are interesting. Chapter 6 of this book is devoted to Parelli's methods.

Classical Riding

I was saddened to hear Monty's views on some of the classical masters. The vehemence and strength of feeling with which he deplores the use of force and cruel methods towards horses is very moving. I am sure that he is absolutely sincere, and I admire him immensely for never being afraid to say what he thinks in defence of horses. I am very pleased, though, that Monty recognises the very good and gentle horsemanship of Sylvia Loch.

I do not know which of the classical masters he has studied, but if their methods were brutal, then they should not be called classical. Since Xenophon wrote in his book *The Art of Horsemanship* in 400BC 'Anything which is forced or misunderstood can never be beautiful' (and these sentiments were reiterated in different ways throughout his book), I can hardly believe that 2,400 years later we are still having this debate. I can, however, believe that Monty has seen displays of extreme brutality from trainers who call themselves 'classical'.

It would be naive to believe that all trainers calling themselves 'classical', throughout the centuries and now for that matter, have adhered to the true classical principles of patience and kindness. I dare say, in most centres of excellence, there may have been riders who have strayed from the correct path and employed brutal methods. I do not doubt that Monty could take me to some places on the European continent where the training methods would make me weep, but that should not be allowed to overshadow the wonderful horsemanship and knowledge that is available to us from the great masters. I wish that he had encountered more of the real masters. If only their knowledge could be combined with his, the result would be spectacular.

'the strength of feeling with which he deplores the use of force is very moving'

Suitability of All Horses for Join-Up

I fully appreciate Monty's response to my question concerning the suitability of all horses for join-up, and acknowledge that it must be very frustrating for him to be asked questions like this. To him, the use of join-up and the Equus language is just a natural way to communicate with horses, and why should anyone not wish to use this communication? It seems the height of rudeness for us to ignore the horse's language, particularly when someone has revealed it to us in such a succinct way.

However, I do have some serious concerns about the use of join-up by the average horse owner for all categories of horse. One category of horse for which I am concerned about using join-up is the aged, possibly arthritic, horse. While these horses may benefit from gentle, relaxed circle work on the lunge, or long-reining, the join-up technique does, of necessity, scare the horse into flight mode initially. Rushing around a relatively small round pen in flight, for an aged horse, could lead to injuries such as tendon or joint strain. Sudden stops and sudden turns for aged horses should also be avoided. I believe, therefore, that anyone about to try join-up for the first time with an elderly horse, or one who has sustained tendon or other injuries in the past, should consider these potential risks.

A Special Connection with Horses

Monty Roberts has brought to the world of horsemanship a knowledge of the horse's own language which, as far as I am aware, has never been understood to this extent before. Some of the Native Americans have had an understanding of the body language of the horse and the interactions within a herd of wild horses, but nobody has ever devised a way of translating this into human body language and utilizing this language in the way that Monty has. He has shown us that young, wild horses can be backed in a relatively stress-free way in a matter of about half an hour, instead of the weeks of painstaking work that was hitherto needed, or indeed the brutal methods of literally 'breaking' the horse. Throughout history, man has needed to back horses quickly, as often large numbers of horses were needed for battle. If only Monty Roberts' methods had been known then, thousands of horses could have been saved incalculable suffering. I also believe that Monty has a very special personal connection with horses. They immediately seem to be at ease with him, and I am sure that they sense the very real love that he has in his heart for them.

'young, wild horses can be backed in a stress-free way instead of the brutal methods of literally 'breaking' the horse'

CHAPTER 8

Sylvia Stanier LVO

A Comprehensive Equestrian Career

*'I prefer to keep to my tried and tested methods,
but am happy to use bonding and holistics if they
complement my methods'*

S ylvia Stanier was born in Gibraltar in 1928, where her father was Military Secretary to two Governors. Her riding career started as a child, and she went on to be taught by the famous show hack trainer, Sam Marsh. During the war, she rode and drove horses. After the war, she did one season in a National Hunt yard from 1949–1950, after which she then went to Ireland. Her time in Ireland was spent working for the Hume Dudgeon family at the Burton Hall Establishment until 1975, the last seven years of which were in the capacity of Chief Instructor.

An Extensive Career

In 1964, 1968 and 1972, Sylvia was an Assistant Trainer to the US Olympic Equestrian Team and has been the winner of many Show Hunter Championships at the Royal Dublin Society's Horse Show. Studying with Einar Schmit Jensen (a trainer at Burton Hall), she learned the Danish method of long-reining, which in fact asks the horse only for the same movements as he would perform while ridden. 1966 saw Sylvia give a brilliant exhibition of long-reining at the Horse of the Year Show at Wembley.

Sylvia's side-saddle career was started by lessons from her mother and continued with Mrs Doreen Archer Houblon. The show jumping side of her career has also been extensive, studying with Colonel Joe Dudgeon covering both the Italian and English systems.

In 1963, Sylvia was appointed as Assistant to Patricia Galvin for her Olympic dressage horses. It was after her long-reinging exhibition at Wembly that she was appointed to ride and assist with Her Majesty the Queen's famous horse Burmese, and other horses, for the ceremony of Trooping the Colour between 1968 and 1986, for which she was appointed a Lieutenant of the Royal Victorian Order.

From 1970 to 1990, Sylvia worked as a Fédération Equestre Internationale (FEI) dressage judge.

Her Work Today

The author of a number of books on equitation, Sylvia is a trainer of international renown. Her career has been nothing short of glittering, and she is very active in the equestrian world at the moment as a freelance trainer and writer.

'her career has been nothing short of glittering ...'

QUESTION 1: *You have trained many of the Queen's horses, including the famous Burmese, the horse ridden side-saddle by the Queen for so many years at ceremonial events. For how many years did you act in this capacity for Her Majesty?*

SYLVIA' REPLY: I helped with the ceremonial horses for the ceremony of Trooping the Colour for 18 years, specifically to train several each year for side-saddle riding.

QUESTION 2: *At what age did you start the horse's training for the Royal ceremonial duties?*

SYLVIA'S REPLY: Most of the horses were broken-in at two to three years in the ordinary manner. Some were home-bred, and some came via the Metropolitan Mounted Police. Those with suitable temperaments were introduced to traffic, bands, and other 'nuisances' at Windsor Castle or Imber Court, where there is plenty of space to accustom the young horse gradually. Those who still seemed suitable were brought to London at approximately five years of age, either to the Royal Mews, Buckingham Palace, or Hyde Park Police Barracks, (also because it is relatively quiet there). The home-breds at the Royal Mews were exercised in the indoor riding school there and also in Hyde Park judiciously. These young horses were gradually, and from a distance, introduced to royal processions, probably after approximately six months in London, graduating to bigger processions after about 12 to 18 months, in other words aged approximately six years. It takes from three to five years to fully train a ceremonial horse.

QUESTION 3: *Is there a predominant breed used for these royal duties and where do they come from?*

SYLVIA'S REPLY: The bays are predominantly Cleveland Bays and Oldenburgs, although Philippa (Prince Philip's charger) is Irish Draught cross Thoroughbred; the Windsor greys predominantly Oldenburgs or Irish Draught.

QUESTION 4: *In your capacity as a classical riding trainer, do you find that the standard of riding in the UK has become better or worse over the past ten to fifteen years?*

SYLVIA'S REPLY: Considering the number of people riding these days, the overall standard of riding is pretty good, particularly at riding-club level. At the higher standards of eventing and show jumping, British riders are amongst the best in the world. The Grand Prix dressage riders are not far behind. An immense amount of money and energy has been poured into equestrianism, especially through sponsorship, and continental trainers have contributed through excellent clinics.

QUESTION 5: *What do you think of the current competitive scene in the UK, in terms of the welfare of the horse?*

SYLVIA'S REPLY: I think the welfare of horses is especially good these days.

QUESTION 6: *Do you think that organizations such as the Classical Riding Club are having a positive effect on riding and the well being of horses in the UK?*

SYLVIA'S REPLY: The Classical Riding Club is an expanding association, which promotes 'better riding', and that can only be a good thing.

QUESTION 7: *What do you think of the current trend of people devising new systems of equine training, which they call 'natural'? I refer here to such things as the work of the 'horse whisperers' and the process of join-up.*

SYLVIA'S REPLY: Personally, I prefer to keep to my tried and tested methods, but am happy to use bonding and holistics if they complement, but do not replace, my basic methods.

QUESTION 8: *Do you think that people are ignoring the classical principles as set out in your two books* The Art of Lungeing *and* The Art of Long Reining, *as well as in* Classical Circus Equitation *by H.J. Lijsen, edited by yourself, in favour of less well tried and tested methods, as advocated by many new trainers?*

SYLVIA'S REPLY: I think that everyday riders simply do not know the original cavalry methods.

QUESTION 9: *Why do you think that so many people have no understanding of simple weight aids, which seems so natural to a true classical rider?*

SYLVIA'S REPLY: My answer here is simple – ignorance.

Robin Porter RVM

A Kindness and Reward Approach

During the time that Sylvia Stanier was appointed to help with the training of the royal horses for the ceremony of Trooping the Colour (from 1968 to 1986), including the side-saddle training of the Queen's horse Burmese, Sylvia latterly received assistance from Sgt. Robin Porter.

Robin was born into a non-equestrian background in London in November 1936. He was called up for national service in 1954, where he chose to serve his term in the Military Police, with the aim of joining the Metropolitan Police on demobilization. After an initial three years in the Metropolitan Police, he applied and was accepted into the Mounted Branch, and was promoted to Sergeant in 1970. After several mounts stationed across central London, he was asked to take charge of Burmese, the Queen's ceremonial horse and a gift to her from the Royal Canadian Mounted Police. He cared for her for 12 years, which resulted in the award of the Royal Victorian Medal (RVM), for services to Her Majesty, in 1987.

On retirement from the Metropolitan Police after 30 years of service, he became the Deputy Chief Field Officer for the International League for the Protection of Horses (ILPH), retiring once again in 2000 after 12 years of service.

Because of Robin Porter's wide experience of training (although he does not describe himself as a trainer, which is typical of his humility), riding and equine welfare knowledge, I am sure that readers will find his views in the following interview very interesting.

QUESTION 1: *I understand that you were in the Mounted Police Force before you became involved in the training of the Queen's ceremonial horses. Did the training of the latter differ greatly from general police horse training?*

ROBIN'S REPLY: I was never, in the strictest sense of the word, a horse trainer, either for the police or for the Queen. I was a police sergeant responsible for the daily operational work of the mounted officers in my charge – work that included street patrols, crowd control and ceremonial duties.

All mounted officers were sent on training courses annually. These were carried out at the Metropolitan Mounted Branch Training Centre at Imber Court. On division in central London, one day per week was set aside for mounted drill, where faults in both horse and rider were corrected.

QUESTION 2: *In what capacity did you train the Queen's horses?*

ROBIN'S REPLY: For most of my 30 years of service, I have been involved with the royal household by providing police horses for royalty to ride on ceremonial and state occasions. These were horses that were considered best suited to the job, in other words in both looks and temperament. Operationally, they were mainly used for traffic and crowd control and for military band escort.

I was asked to look after Burmese in the late 1970s, as it was thought that her talents were wasted as a simple riding hack. Being stabled at Rochester Row in central London, Her Majesty could ride her whenever she was in town and if required at Windsor, it was an easy box ride.

QUESTION 3: *Did you ride Burmese side-saddle and if so, did you find this difficult compared with riding astride?*

ROBIN'S REPLY: I was lucky to have Burmese for about 12 years, and during that time rode her in every facet of police work. She had been trained by the Royal Canadian Mounted Police (RCMP) and was always happiest when leading from the front. On the occasions when Her Majesty rode side-saddle, I would try it myself while preparing Burmese. Though so different from astride, I did not find it difficult, but felt more in control when riding astride.

'horses do not have the ability to reason and are happiest being told what to do'

QUESTION 4: *Do you think that if some of the modern training methods had been better known then – such as Monty Robert's join-up technique – they would have been of benefit to use with the horses that you trained?*

ROBIN'S REPLY: In the training of police horses, kindness and reward have always been paramount. In my experience, where any form of training involves force or cruelty, the result is always failure. Horses that are treated with respect and kindness respond better in all manner of ways, for example, in confidence and health. I am of the opinion that a lot of Monty Roberts' techniques were being used before he came on the scene. The breaking and training of police horses has changed very little over the years and has evolved into a tried and tested formula – kindness and reward.

QUESTION 5: *Do you think that schooling horses on the lunge is beneficial for the horse?*

ROBIN'S REPLY: I think the lunge is of huge benefit to both horse and rider. In training, it is essential for getting the animal correct in balance and pace without a rider and for the rider to settle a horse prior to riding. I have used the lunge to great effect over the years.

QUESTION 6: *Do you think that the horse/human relationship should be a 50/50 balance, or would you say that the human should hold the balance of power and responsibility?*

ROBIN'S REPLY: In the horse/human relationship, the human should most definitely hold the balance of power and responsibility. Horses do not have the ability to reason and are happiest when being told what to do. Any other consideration is courting disaster.

QUESTION 7: *What do you think of the current trend towards 'new' and 'natural' training methods, such as Parelli Natural Horsemanship?*

ROBIN'S REPLY: I am not against trying any 'new' or 'natural' training methods providing key elements are not excluded, ie reward and kindness. I am a traditionalist and prefer tried and tested methods.

QUESTION 8 : *Do you think that people nowadays are ignoring the classical principles in favour of less well tried and tested methods as advocated by many 'new' trainers?*

ROBIN'S REPLY: Results are always the measure of success of any method in training. From what I can see, the old principles still work and I have no evidence that new methods are having any greater success.

QUESTION 9: *In your capacity as a Field Officer for the International League for the Protection of Horses, do you consider that the welfare of equines in the UK is improving or deteriorating?*

ROBIN'S REPLY: Having worked in equine welfare for the International League for the Protection of Horses (ILPH) for 12 years, I would say that the general level of equine welfare has remained static during that time. Public awareness is greater now than when I first started, but ignorance is still a major factor now, as it was then. There are some awful people out there, though thankfully they are in the minority.

Welfare organizations have improved, and liaison is much better between them. Cruelty will always exist, and hopefully the net will tighten on the perpetrators. With organizations like the ILPH working together for ever-increasing levels of public awareness, it will hopefully mean that many of these beautiful creatures will not suffer because of a lack of interest in reporting cases to the authorities.

Summary and Conclusions

Despite his vast achievements and experience, Robin Porter is one of the most humble people I have met. He is, in my opinion, another example of one of the best traditional British horsemen. Having cared for the Queen's horse and also been an ILPH field officer, he must have seen the best and the worst of horse welfare in the UK, and yet he is very practical and non-judgemental, always wishing to educate people in better ways to care for their horses.

'cruelty will always exist, and hopefully the net will tighten on the perpetrators'

CHAPTER 9

Linda Tellington-Jones

A True Holistic Approach

*'The aim is to improve the horse's entire well being,
including his mind, body and spirit'*

Linda Tellington-Jones has devised what she calls the TTouch and TTeam training system. Linda is a Canadian trainer, who developed her system over a period of some 25 years. She developed the TTeam first, and the TTouch followed on a few years later. Although they were first used in the USA, the TTeam training method and TTouch therapy are now widely used all over the world.

The Tellington Touch System is very successful and popular, and was devised before the onset of most of the 'new' and 'natural' training methods. It is a system that is used in every type of discipline with any type or breed of horse. It is valuable for any horse, but is particularly valuable for those with problems such as napping, rearing, bolting, refusal to load and so on. Several of the modern trainers whose methods I have studied for this book, including Kelly Marks, have told me that they have been influenced by Linda Tellington-Jones.

TTeam is an acronym for Tellington Touch Equine Awareness Method. The aim of this method is to improve the horse's entire well being, including his mind, body and spirit. It consists mainly of a type of massage system, using various circular motions and strokes with the hands on different parts of the horse's body to help with different problems. Although this is more of a therapy than a training system, and might therefore not appear immediately to come under the scope of this book, I am nevertheless including a short description of the TTouches. Not only are the TTouches fascinating, but they are integral to the training system – a true holistic approach. In fact TTouches are seen as a way of supporting most training methods. They are used to encourage relaxation and improve athletic ability, as well as to promote a sense of mutual awareness between horse and rider.

Linda uses varying degrees of hand pressure, and various sizes of circles and strokes, as well as varying speeds of movement with the hands – all for differing purposes. Each different type of stroke is light-heartedly named after an animal. For instance, the basic

'each different type of stroke is light-heartedly named after an animal'

TTouch is a circular movement called the Clouded Leopard TTouch. This is a TTouch which can be used to encourage the horse to lower his head when mounted. Linda describes how the rider can reach out and do this TTouch on the crest of his neck, close to his poll. It is also used from the ground as a request for the horse to lower his head.

TTouches done in and around the horse's mouth are said to help with various problems such as resistance, nervousness, teeth grinding and so on. Linda says that they can be very helpful in the case of horses who bite, that they are almost always a cure.

Linda has devised an unusual way of helping horses who are in pain with colic. This can be done while waiting for the vet to arrive. Basically, you take a large bath towel and fold it to about five inches (12cm) in width. Place one end over the horse's back and take the other end around under the belly, as if it were a girth. Then, keeping your top hand still, very gently and slowly raise the lower end of the towel. If the horse accepts this, the position should be kept for about six seconds, and then very slowly released until the towel is loose (taking about twice the time as you held the lift). This, combined with ear TTouches, should relieve the pain until the vet arrives.

This belly lift is not only for relief of pain, but is designed to help with horses who object to having their girth tightened, are 'cold-backed', or who buck when first mounted.

'the horse is made more aware of his own body and how he can use it…'

The following is a very brief outline of these techniques, and I would strongly advise anyone interested in practising them to read Linda's book *Improve Your Horse's Well-Being* (Kenilworth Press 1999) and/or learn from a TTeam instructor or practitioner. There are also many Tellington Touch videos available for further learning (see page 142).

Combining Classical Riding with the Feldenkrais Method

Linda's methods were originally based on a combination of classical riding and the Feldenkrais method. (A short description of the Feldenkrais Method – which is used by many riders to increase awareness of their action – is given in Chapter 10). A few years after the introduction of her TTeam work, Linda introduced her TTouch method in 1983. She tells us that her interest in cellular intelligence and equine massage helped lead to the Tellington TTouch. TTeam work and TTouches are closely linked to one another.

Many of the Tellington Touches have a dual purpose, not only for remedial therapy to improve behavioural and/or physical problems, but also to make the horse more aware of his own body and how he can use it. In this way, the Tellington Touches can be used as training aids.

Hind-Leg Circles

For instance, hind-leg circles are designed to bring about evenness of gait, as well as helping the horse to understand how he can move his hind legs to the front and side. This should have the effect of helping him to execute lateral work, as well as helping his balance when standing for the farrier.

The Body Wrap and Rope

Another unusual technique used by Linda is the Body Wrap and Rope, which she describes as TTeam training tools. The Body Wrap is basically two elastic bandages joined together. One bandage goes around the horse's neck. The other goes around the hindquarters, and they are joined together. The Rope is virtually the same as the Wrap, but made of strong, soft nylon tied in a figure-of-eight around the horse's body. I will not describe the fitting of these in any more detail, since anyone wishing to use them would be wise to seek assistance from a TTeam trainer.

The Wrap and Rope are used for various purposes and can be used when riding or during groundwork. One reason for using the Wrap or Rope would be to achieve a more balanced stance and improve the horse's topline, making him look 'rounder'. If it actually helps the horse to use himself in a correct way without force, then I would certainly be in favour of it.

'the Wrap and Rope give horses confidence when entering confined spaces…'

However, I have my suspicions that some people may expect this 'rounder' appearance almost immediately. In fact, this is almost certain to be the interpretation by many inexperienced horse owners. If this is the case, then, in my opinion, it is a false 'quick fix'.

I do not believe that this would be Linda's intention, but it is an unfortunate fact of life these days when people are, to my mind, obsessed by the horse's 'outline'. I firmly believe that what the great masters have told us through the centuries is true. In other words, a 'round outline' can come only from slow and steady classical exercises to build the strength and flexibility in the hind limbs and back muscles, thus enabling the horse to lighten the forehand and take more weight on his quarters.

The Wrap and Rope are also designed for other purposes such as to give the horse confidence when entering confined spaces and to help those who shy. Providing that these Wraps and Ropes are not so tight as to force the horse into moving in a certain way, I can see no harm at all in their use. If they are found to give confidence to a nervous horse, then that's great.

Groundwork

Chain Lead Line

A chain lead line is used for groundwork. This is a lead line with a portion of chain and a clip at one end. A Tellington lead rope is necessary for use in conjunction with this. The instructions for fitting this lead line are very precise, and I would suggest anyone wishing to use one should consult a TTeam consultant or practitioner. Linda does point out that leading from both sides is beneficial.

The Zephyr Lead

For people who are unsure about using a chain, or for young sensitive horses, Linda advises the use of the Zephyr lead. This is similar to the chain lead described above, but utilizes a piece of soft rope instead of the chain.

The Wand

Linda uses a whip – preferably white – which she calls a 'wand' and the horse can be asked to move towards it. She describes how to teach your horse to walk towards you, from right to left in front of you, to halt, and to walk over obstacles such as plastic sheets and wooden see-saws. She also uses it to tap the horse gently to encourage him to move forwards and, in true classical fashion, she so rightly calls it an extension to the trainer's arm.

Lungeing

Linda lunges horses slightly differently from traditional methods. She lunges on an oval, initially with an ordinary lead rope and a wand – the trainer walking with the horse. She devised this method to help regain the confidence of horses who had been frightened away with the whip. If the horse is particularly nervous, then two people walk either side of the horse, until he gradually builds confidence. This seems an excellent way to teach the horse to walk while keeping a specified distance from the handler. It is obviously not lungeing, but at this stage it is not intended to be. Not until the horse has learned, and is confident with, the basic walk and halt commands would Linda revert to a lunge rein of traditional length, of say 30 feet (9m), and commence trot work. The horse is not on a consistent bend as he would be on a circle. It is this constant circle work that I believe Linda is aiming to avoid, since she has witnessed the damage of bad lungeing, where the horse is sent around too fast, on too small a circle, for too long a duration.

I think that this is a very valid groundwork exercise. My only concern is that some people may not be agile enough to move around quickly, and in the faster paces of say canter, the horse could be asked to perform too tight a turn. We come back to the principle that any method can be detrimental if not carried out properly. Just as many people misuse traditional lungeing techniques, Linda's way of lungeing could be very helpful or detrimental, depending on the ability of the trainer. (See Chapter 12, General Issues and Conclusions, for more advice on lungeing techniques.)

'having to concentrate on where to place their feet has a calming effect on most horses'

The Labyrinth

This is a series of ground poles, each 12 feet (3.6m) long. They are placed in such a way as to make a type of maze. Linda describes how to teach your horse to walk around the poles, thus facilitating balance, coordination and awareness of where and how the horse is placing himself. The horse can also be asked to step over the poles. This is a particularly useful exercise for horses who are unbalanced and also for nervous or easily distracted ones. The necessity to concentrate on where they are placing their feet seems to have a calming effect on most horses. It can also help to teach a horse to lower his head and use his back rather than move with a hollowed back.

The Star, Cavaletti and Pick-up Sticks

The Star is a fan configuration of four twelve-foot (3.6m) long heavy poles with an object such as a straw bale at one end to place the end of the poles upon. To begin with, Linda advises that we should start with the poles on the ground about four feet (1.2m) apart at the wide end. Once your horse is familiar with this exercise, you can raise one end of the poles on the bale as suggested. You should adjust the distance and height of the poles to suit your horse. At first, you should lead the horse over the lowest point. The trainer should be walking on the inside; in other words at a higher point than the horse, and walking two poles in front of him, thus giving him a lead and an opportunity to judge the height and distance of the poles. When the horse is completely at ease with this exercise, you can progress to gradually walking him deeper in the Star.

When he becomes really adept at this, you can challenge him even more by raising some of the poles, making them uneven heights, and/or moving the poles closer together. Obviously, this should be done tactfully and very gradually. Linda points out that you should be sure to lead your horse from both sides and in both directions. She also advises that you lead him using TTouch positions such as Grace of the Cheetah, Dolphin Flickering Through the Waves, and Flight of the Eagle positions. I do not propose to describe these in depth. I think it would be far preferable that you seek instruction from a qualified TTeam practitioner or instructor.

The Pick-up Sticks are a slight variation on the above exercise in that the poles are laid down in a 'slightly organized mess'. The aim is to create different-sized spaces for your horse to step into. You must be sure, however, that they are not too high and cannot be rolled over if they are knocked.

The work over cavaletti is not dissimilar to the traditional use of these obstacles, except that Linda advises walking with the horse over them, instead of actually jumping them. The use of cavaletti as jumping obstacles has largely been abandoned in latter years, because of the safety aspect. Obviously they are solid, and will not fall if hit by the horse, and, in the event of an accident, the wooden crosses at the ends could make very nasty impaling sticks.

'in Pick-up Sticks, the poles are laid down in a slightly organized mess'

However, used in the way that Linda is advocating, I can see no problem with them – providing of course that the horse remains calm. They can be used in a variety of different positions, creating differing heights, by simply turning them over so that the longer-end cross-members rest on the floor.

The Bridge, Teeter-Totter (See-Saw) and Platform

These are all fairly self-explanatory. Apart from the see-saw, they are obstacles that most horses in the UK face every day. The need to walk over wooden bridges and onto wooden platforms over ditches is a common requirement in our bridleway network. I found her advice on how to teach your horse to negotiate these obstacles extremely sound and kind. For instance, if he refuses to walk onto the platform, you can place a little feed on the wood. She also describes here how other TTouches will help the horse to accept the situation calmly. I have always realised that food is not only a good bribe in these circumstances, but it does, in fact, have a calming effect on the horse. Here is what Linda has to say on this issue:

'When a horse is afraid – of these exercises, or any others – the use of food is an excellent idea. When a horse eats, the para-sympathetic nervous system is activated, and this overrides the sympathetic nervous system which instigates the flight reaction.' (*Improve Your Horse's Well-Being*)

The see-saw exercise is obviously a step further from the bridge and platform. The horse may well be startled at first when the platform moves under his feet, so he must be very confident before being faced with this. This is an obstacle that

'when a horse is afraid, the use of food is an excellent idea'

is used in such disciplines as Working Equitation, which is a competitive sport recently introduced into the UK and originating from Portugal. It incorporates various classical movements as well as obstacles such as the see-saw. It is obviously not a new idea, but the way in which Linda trains the horse to overcome his natural fear is brilliant.

Working with Plastic Sheets

Linda describes how first to teach your horse to walk through a gap with two pieces of plastic sheet on either side of him in a 'V' shape. Once he can do this confidently, you move the sheets closer together, until eventually he will walk over the sheets where they join at the 'V' end.

If your horse is afraid to walk through water, you can incorporate water onto the plastic. This seems to me to be a brilliant idea, if it is all done gradually and systematically.

The next step is to ask him to walk in between two upright rails covered in plastic sheets. After that, he can be taught to walk underneath plastic. Linda describes how, with the use of two helpers, you can first encourage him to walk under two wands held up over the top of him. Once he gets used to that, you can progress to plastic sheets. At first you start with them held high, but when he is confident, they can actually brush over his back. Linda describes what to do if things go wrong, and it is all done in a very sensible and kind fashion, and must be a great help and confidence giver for teaching the horse to load into a horse box.

Summary and Conclusions

Perhaps the most interesting part of Linda's system is the Tellington Touches. Anything that can help a horse to relax or to help him to be more dextrous is certainly a wonderful thing and needs to be explored to the full, and I find it fascinating. Linda's development of groundwork exercises is certainly innovative. I believe her Labyrinth system to be unique. To combine these excellent ideas with the TTouches to help the horse even more is certainly a new way to approach the training of the horse. The therapy really is part of the training. In the Tellington system, the two are intrinsically intertwined to form the whole system. As mentioned previously, I know that Linda's work has influenced many of our modern trainers. I can see the similarity in many of the groundwork exercises. This, in my opinion, can only be a good thing.

'anything that can help a horse to relax or to be more dextrous is certainly a wonderful thing...'

CHAPTER 10

The Feldenkrais Method

Teaching Efficient Action

*'The aim is a body that is organized to move with minimal
effort and maximum efficiency, not through muscular
strength, but increased consciousness of how it works'*
Moshe Feldenkrais (1904–1984)

Many riders today are, like Linda Tellington-Jones, turning to the method devised by Dr. Moshe Feldenkrais, who, as well as being a renowned physicist was also a mechanical engineer and an expert in judo. He came upon the system after sustaining a knee injury himself. At first, he merely observed his own habitual movement patterns and then set about finding different ways of moving in order to lessen the impact of his injured knee. Finding that this was successful in helping him to overcome his injury, he then applied the principles to other people with differing problems.

The Feldenkrais method teaches people to be aware of their own 'action' ie their movements. It may be surprising to learn that most of us are not aware of what our bodies are doing because habitual movements are 'ingrained' in our nervous systems. On this basis, the Feldenkrais method sets about teaching people more 'efficient' patterns of movement which can be 'ingrained' in the nervous system to replace the 'inefficent' or less useful patterns of movements which may have been inadvertently learned over a period of many years. The Feldenkrais method consists of non-strenuous, gentle lessons designed to promote body awareness.

'evenness of the rider is at the core of good riding'

Many riders are undoubtedly hampering their horses every day – albeit unwittingly. This is obvious to any riding teacher worth their salt. If a rider is not sitting square on the horse, in other words with the weight evenly balanced on either seat bone, how can the poor horse possibly be balanced and perform equally in either direction? This is an aspect of riding that is all too often neglected in many riding lessons. Unevenness is usually blamed on the horse. However, I consider that evenness of the rider is at the core of good riding.

Helping the Collapsed Hip

Putting the matter right if there is a problem is sometimes not easy. The worst scenario that I have come across is the collapsed hip – when the rider is sitting much deeper in the saddle on one seat bone. The rider is often genuinely unaware of this, and I would applaud any method that can help in this direction. Often the rider has been riding with one stirrup longer than the other for some considerable time, believing that they have odd-length legs. Obviously, the balance of the saddle on the horse's back must also be checked in case this is contributing to the problem.

The reason I say that the collapsed hip is the worst scenario is that quite often, even when this fault is pointed out and accepted by the rider, the rider is quite incapable of rectifying the situation. This is usually because of an out-of-balance pelvis. The pelvis may have been pulled or pushed 'out-of-true' during an accident, or may have become unbalanced slowly over a long period of time due to everyday life, such as lifting heavy objects, bad posture and so on. However, help is at hand – a good chiropractor or other professional can usually put the matter right, and if not immediately, after a few treatments. I have a personal liking for McTimoney Chiropractic as it is so gentle yet effective. I have also had great results with 'hands-on' energy healing.

If you are worried that your pelvis may not be straight, check whether your legs are the same length! It is possible that you could have been born with one leg longer than the other, but much more probable that your pelvis has become 'out-of-true'. If it has happened slowly, then the chances are that your body has just got used to it or, as Dr. Feldenkrais puts it, 'your posture has become ingrained on your nervous system'. Obviously, if the rider is not balanced, then the horse will not be. However, once this is corrected, the horse can then start to correct his way of going.

Addressing Other Postural Problems

The Feldenkrais method can help to lessen and even eradicate many other postural and movement problems such as poor head posture, stiff shoulders, arms and wrists. The thigh, knee, lower leg and ankle can also cause problems for riders.

To make people more aware of what their bodies are doing is totally in tune with classical principles. This method can help people to learn the correct use of the spine, thus enabling them to guide the horse and absorb the movement. It is also of particular help to anyone after an illness or injury, as well as immense help to anyone suffering from hereditary postural problems. It often helps people with emotional problems, since it creates self-confidence and self-reliance as well as promoting a general feeling of well-being.

One further method which is often mentioned in combination with the Feldenkrais method is the Alexander Technique.

'most of us are not aware of what our bodies are doing…'

This is a system of relaxation and controlled breathing, which promotes well-being and good posture and is often used hand-in-hand with the Feldenkrais approach. Much of the Alexander technique is carried out in what is called 'the semi-supine position', which basically requires the person to lie on their back on the floor, with a small head support of, say, a small cushion, with the knees bent and raised. Alexander technicians tell us that this position is one of mechanical advantage for the spine and can be of enormous benefit for people suffering from backaches, stress and so on. For instance, as we breath out, we should have a feeling of the whole spine lengthening in an upward direction from the seat bones. The technique gives a good feeling of how the pelvis and spine provide a core support and balance for the torso. This idea could be most helpful if transferred to horse riding. While practising the Alexander Technique, one can learn how to allow the spine and leg to lengthen by freeing the neck. This is encouraged by way of thought patterns. The upward and outward feel of the torso is very helpful, as is the idea that the seat bones are rockers, on which one could allow the movement of the horse.

Summary and Conclusions

The Feldenkrais method *can* be learned through books and videos, but by far the best way to start learning, as with most methods, is 'real life' lessons, either in a group or a private lesson situation. Within the Feldenkrais method, there are two techniques – 'awareness through movement' which is used in groups, and 'functional integration', which is used in private individual lessons. There are also Feldenkrais rider-related days, weekends and events happening throughout the year. The best way to find the whereabouts of your nearest event would be to contact an alternative training centre or see page 142 for further information. In addition, organizations such as the Classical Riding Club usually have someone amongst their membership who has an interest in this method and can put you on the right path.

'the Feldenkrais method can help to lessen and even eradicate many movement problems'

CHAPTER 11

Doma Vaquera

A Sport of Agility and Skill

*'Very accurate body posture and changes-of-weight
aids from the rider achieve all the movements'*

Although Doma Vaquera is a sport and not a specific system of training, it is included here because it is a sport which is fast growing in popularity world-wide, and I am sure that readers will want to be clear as to what it is all about. Sylvia Loch has made reference to Doma Vaquera in her interview in chapter 2.

Not surprisingly, it is already very popular in Spain, its country of origin, and has become a major sport in such countries as France and Italy. It has a growing following in the USA and has recently been introduced to the UK. These are just some of the countries where it is practised; a list of Doma Vaquera Societies are included in the Useful Addresses on page 142.

Many people are under the impression that Doma Vaquera emanates from the bull-fighting ring, but this is not quite true. The sport comes from the Iberian peninsular, emanating from the everyday work of the Portuguese, the Spanish and, later, the Argentinians. The word 'vaquera' loosely translated means 'cowboy'. The Spanish vaqueros had to work with cattle out on the plains and obviously, there were bulls within these herds. If they needed to single out and catch an individual cow, then they would have to ride with both reins in one hand; in the other hand, they would hold a garrocha, which is a 14–16 foot-long (4-5m) pole, which was used to knock down the cow.

'skill and finesse on the part of the rider, as well as athleticism of the horse, are required'

Skill, Speed and Agility

From the skill of these working practices, the sport of Doma Vaquera was born. As if 'catching' a cow this way were not difficult enough, they often had to contend with an angry bull. Iberian fighting bulls can be very mean to people and horses! This is where the real skill, speed and agility of horse and rider are a matter of life and death. To enable them to escape the horns of the bull, the horse was required to perform speedy half-passes, canter pirouettes, fast halts, rein backs, to name just a few of the movements.

Most of these movements can also be seen in Grand Prix dressage, the difference being that dressage riders may use both hands on the reins and are not, of necessity, in such a hurry!

The Doma Vaquera Association of Spain was incorporated in 1972, making regulations for formal competition, and, in recent years, the competition has been brought to the UK. The British representative for the Association is Richard Lüst, who is the founder of the British Doma Vaquera Association. Richard has also represented Great Britain in the Doma Vaquera European Championships. The 2002 qualifying rounds were held in France.

Basically this sport is comprised of all lateral work, half-passes, full-passes, rein-back, demi-pirouettes and canter-pirouettes on each rein, two turns on the forehand and two turns on the haunches, large and small circles, flying changes, figures of eight across the arena, counter-canter and canter half-passes – all completed in walk, working canter and gallop. There is no trot work allowed in the competition: only walk, canter and gallop, and half the competition is carried out in walk. The vaqueros no longer have to hold a garrocha, but must ride with only one hand on the reins, holding the other hand gracefully in front of their torso.

The competition tests last for seven minutes, and the movements can be ridden in any sequence.

The bits used for this work are, understandably, quite severe, but should be used with such light hands from the rider that the horses' mouths should never be hurt. Richard Lüst points out that it is not the same as American cowboy 'neck-reining'. Anyone who jabs a horse in the mouth or hurts his horse with a spur during competition is immediately disqualified. Very accurate body posture and changes-of-weight aids from the rider achieve all the movements.

This competitive sport is fast growing world-wide, but 2002 was the first time that we had a British contender in the European Championships.

Needless to say, to perform Doma Vaquera, the horse has to be working well from behind, and to be going well forward, as you would expect in an advanced dressage test. If you get the chance to see a Doma Vaquera competition, it certainly is an exciting spectator sport. It is not strictly 'classical', but it certainly requires a high degree of skill and finesse on the part of the rider, as well as athleticism of the horse.

Many of the horses used are full- and part-bred Spanish, but also Anglo Arabs, Trés Sangres (Anglo Hispano-Arab, ie Spanish x Anglo-Arab), and (perhaps surprisingly) British Thoroughbreds. All breeds are allowed in the competition.

Summary and Conclusions

As mentioned previously, Doma Vaquera is not strictly classical. Some of the movements are carried out at high speed and, personally, I find that this loses some of the beauty and grace of true classical riding. Also, it includes movements that are not classical – an example being fast, long, rein-backs, which are not part of a classical training system, but which may be an important requirement when escaping the horns of a raging bull! Conversely, having said this, I find that Doma Vaquera can be absolutely breathtaking in its own way when well ridden. Many times I have stood in wonder at the skill of Richard Lüst. He merely appears to think sideways and the horse goes that way. There are often no visible leg or rein aids. When ridden correctly in this way, the horses are certainly not receiving any jabs or discomfort from the aids; this is a lot more than can be said for many Grand Prix dressage riders, not to mention polo riders, show jumpers, or indeed riders in any field!

CHAPTER 12

General Issues
and Conclusions

*'They need to know who owns them, they need a
regular and fair regime where they feel safe and,
dare I say it, they need love'*

The Argument: For and Against Whips

Some modern trainers, including Monty Roberts, are firmly against the use of the whip. Having read his book *The Man Who Listens to Horses*, which tells the story of his life with horses, I can well understand why. His father appeared to be a strict disciplinarian incorporating the worst of the 'old school'. He believed in horses being broken-in using the methods that his ancestors and contemporaries used, which was the 'norm' for many parts of the world. Monty recalls how horses were tied up in such a way that escape was impossible, one leg tied up at a time and then whipped, until they had no fight left in them. To see one's own flesh and blood inflict such abject cruelty must have been absolutely horrendous for him. Bearing in mind that these methods may not have seemed cruel to his father, who was only following tradition, Monty must have been a very sensitive and independent-thinking boy to have realised the cruelty of the situation. It is amazing that he turned out to be such a kind and caring person, and my heart really goes out to him in this respect.

'the use of the whip is a means of communication, not a means to inflict pain'

There are other eminent people at the present time who abhor the use of the whip, their reasoning probably being the same as Monty Roberts' – they have probably seen the whip misused as a means of beating the horse. The trouble with this view is that the use of the whip should NOT be cruel. As we can see from his interview, Monty now appreciates that the whip can be used as an aid in certain circumstances. The great riding masters, throughout the ages, have insisted that it is a means of communication with the horse, not a means to inflict pain. For instance, the Spanish Riding School uses the whip today. When teaching the horse to passage and piaffe in-hand, the trainer uses a tap on the leg by the whip to indicate a higher lifting of that leg. These stallions are neither hurt nor frightened by it. They accept the contact of the whip as it is intended to be – as an extension of the trainer's arm.

The main trouble with a whip is obviously not the whip itself but the person using it. Any piece of equipment can become an object with which to inflict pain in the wrong hands. A snaffle bit can inflict considerable pain when used badly, but this seems to be largely ignored because the pain is not so obvious to the onlooker.

In addition, I think we have a problem with the actual word. The word 'whip' conjures up in the mind the act of inflicting pain and instilling fear in the recipient. It has been used over the centuries as a means of administering punishment to all animals, human and otherwise. Therefore I believe that we should substitute the word whip with a word such as 'feather', because any other term such as rod, cane, prod, pole or stick would also give the idea of pain.

I am not the first person to have had this idea. Linda Tellington-Jones calls her white whip a 'wand', and circus trainers have referred to their whips as 'guiders'.

The whip, or 'feather' as I shall now call it, is there to create a contact point with the horse. A contact can be pleasurable as well as instructive. My own horses appreciate actually being stroked with the feather on their necks. When the feather is lightly touched behind the rider's leg when working, they know that is an encouragement to use their inside hind leg a little more actively. It certainly does not upset them in any way. When bothered by flies when being ridden, my own mare actually stops and turns her head towards me, so that I can wave the feather in front of her face to rid her of a particularly annoying insect. When the waving has created the desired result, she turns her head away and we continue our ride. I would never wish to be without my feather. It is so useful to have this extension to my arm. Incidentally, Monty Roberts actually uses his own 'unique' version of my 'feather' which is shaped just like a human arm and is used to touch the horse in particularly vulnerable areas.

'there are riding schools where the riders, at every stride, are booting the poor horses'

There are hundreds of riding schools in this country where the riders, at every stride, are booting the poor horses. They become what is known as 'dead to the leg'. I believe that the nerve endings can actually be damaged by this continual kicking. At the very least, this can surely lead to areas of hardened skin which are less sensitive. Luckily, given time, patience, and correct riding, sensitivity does, in practice, usually return. But to the uneducated onlooker, kicking seems to be acceptable. Yet if these riders were to take up a feather and give the horse a tap, this would probably be seen as cruel. A quick tap with the whip is so much kinder to teach the horse to go forward from the leg.

People in general need to be re-educated as to the uses and advantages of the feather and to forget all the hitherto aggressive ways of using it.

Nature or Nurture? – The Debate on Horse Management

I think many people nowadays, in an attempt to get 'back to nature', are in danger of looking at the past, and nature itself, through rose-coloured spectacles. I am certainly not saying that we should ignore the horse's natural instincts and needs, and I am in favour of using Mother Nature's remedies whenever possible. However, we must not forget that nature can be cruel. Not every horse is happiest living in a group of several horses. The elderly, or least dominant horse can become seriously bullied. After all, these are the animals who would not 'make it' in the wild. Horses in the wild do not live to great ages – they usually die! Quite often these deaths are prolonged and agonizing.

I see more unhappy horses turned out to grass nowadays than I ever did, say 20 years ago. This, I think, stems from the mistaken belief that horses can never be happy in a stable. This is the currently favoured regime brought about by some well-meaning modern trainers. (Thankfully, not all modern trainers have this belief, as can be seen in the chapters of this book.) We see this message thrust at us from all angles. Practically every horse magazine in each issue tells us to turn our horses out, so that they can 'be horses'. This gives everyday horse owners the impression that they are being cruel if they keep their horses stabled for the majority of the time. There are even competitive riders who keep their horses out at grass all year round, with no rugs, and no shoes. It is true that some horses, usually very hairy ponies, can live out all year happily without rugs, but these hairy ponies who do well out at grass are not usually ridden very often, normally just a hack once or twice a week during winter.

It is a totally different matter when horses are being ridden more regularly and doing faster work, particularly at competitive level. Also, these competition horses tend to be larger animals with more hot blood, such as Thoroughbreds, Thoroughbred crosses or warmbloods, who are far less well equipped to deal with cold, wet weather. If they are not wearing rugs in winter, they will grow a thick winter coat (or as thick as the genetics of their breeding will allow). They will naturally roll in mud, which has to be groomed away, at least from where the tack will be placed (if this does not happen, their backs would become very sore). The process of grooming takes away some of the grease and dirt which is the horse's natural armour against the cold and wet. Then, when they are ridden, if they are not rugged and presumably therefore not clipped (at least one would hope not) and, if they have grown a full winter coat, they are bound to sweat. Apart from the fact of the discomfort at the time (like a human running while wearing an overcoat), the act of sweating robs the horse of more natural grease from the coat, as well as bodily energy, and they lose condition. After their exercise/training session or competition, they may be turned back out, often in appalling weather conditions, when they are probably tired and in the least best condition to cope with it, having lost much of their natural defences against the weather.

'the idea that horses are unhappy while stabled makes me extremely cross'

We must not forget the horse's need for shelter from flies and burning sun in the summer. Trees, unfortunately, do not provide shelter from flies. The vast majority of flies do not go inside a stable or good field shelter.

While I would be the first to say that horses enjoy a time out each day to relax and social-ize with friends, the idea that horses are necessarily unhappy while stabled makes me extremely cross.

Let us consider the horse's history. Yes, they do emanate from free-roaming herd animals, whose means of survival was their ability to flee from predators. They lived in herds because there is safety in numbers. Of course, they have not lost their flight instinct or their ability to function within a herd. Their mental make-up is built around the herd, where each horse has its own place in the hierarchy. Horses build up strong friendship bonds within this hierarchy, and they also have enemies within the herd. In a wild situation, enemies usually keep a wide distance from each other. This is not always possible in a domestic situation.

There are also the horses who are at the bottom of the hierarchy scale, who get pushed around by just about all the other herd members. They survive by being subservient to everyone they encounter, and in this way they manage to stay within the herd. I have observed this type of behaviour in domesticated horses. The trouble is that in a domesticated situation, they do not have a choice of who they should be turned out with. In addition, turn-out paddocks are often not large enough for the poor subservient horse to keep a safe distance away from his enemies. In this way, life can be pretty miserable for the 'under-dog'. I am sure that these horses are really glad when it is time for them to be taken back to the stables – if they are lucky enough.

Obviously, with careful observation and planning, these problems could be overcome, given that there are enough separate paddocks or sufficient space available. Nevertheless, however carefully the horses are chosen to be turned out together, there is always a dominant horse. If there is a field shelter, he will be the one who will use it. He may not stay in there all the time, as he knows he can go back there whenever he wishes. However inclement the weather may be, or however hard the flies may bite, the other horses will not go into the shelter, for fear of being trapped by the dominant horse. Thus has arisen the fallacy that people are so fond of quoting: 'However bad the weather, the horses prefer to stand outside'. Of course horses can survive outside, but surviving is not at all the same as thriving.

Consider this: how many generations ago did the average British riding horse roam free on the plains? Possibly as many generations as our ancestors lived in caves. Are we intending to give up our centrally-heated homes to go back to a more 'natural' life in a cave? Perhaps the competitors keeping their horses out all year with no rugs because it is 'natural' should try a more 'natural' life themselves, before consigning their horses to a permanent outside life where they must battle against the elements. Horses, like us, have evolved through their generations and have adapted and even come to enjoy life with humans, even if it may be in a more artificial environment. We have also 'bred' out of them many of their hardier traits such as long hair and so on.

I certainly accept that many horses are deprived of their social life and should be turned out whenever possible, but to many horses this is not the most important thing in their lives. Obviously, horses showing signs of behavioural distress, such as weaving and wind-sucking, should have their routines seriously re-appraised and altered. However, I would disagree with the popular opinion that vices such as weaving and so on are solely caused by long hours in the stable. I believe that these poor creatures, in most cases, are suffering from a lack of security and stimulation as much as a lack of equine social life. Security for horses in a captive situation can, and usually does, come from their human keepers. They need to know who 'owns' them, they need a regular and fair regime where they feel safe and, dare I say it, they need love. Turning them out with other horses does not always solve the problem.

I spend many hours of contact with my own horses every day, and I know that they

'horses can survive outside, but surviving is not at all the same as thriving'

would definitely not thank me for turning them out in bad weather. As long as they are exercised and have plenty of hay to munch, they are much happier inside, although they do go out whenever the weather permits. If they are out in the field and the weather takes a turn

'…even hairy native ponies appreciate their stables on winter nights'

for the worse, they all stand by the fence calling to me to bring them in, regardless of the time of day. One of my horses, during a thunder storm, when I could not get them all in quickly enough, broke out of the field and came rushing into the yard on his own. As soon as his stable door was opened, he went inside.

Stables should not be dark, miserable places, but places of warmth and comfort, preferably with a nice view and stable companions close by. I strongly believe that horses feel the cold much more than people like to think, and even hairy native ponies appreciate their stables on winter nights, particularly as they grow old. This belief is born out of many years of experience caring for horses, and regularly feeling their ears, which should be warm to the touch. When the ears are wet, this can be deceiving, then a hand under the chest will usually tell you if the horse is cold. Remember that a horse's temperature should be higher than ours (around 100.5°F or 38°C) – so they should feel warm! Of course very cold, still weather is much more bearable – horses hate wet and windy weather, which is much the same as humans really. I can work around the yard in jodhpurs and sweatshirt, without a coat and without feeling the cold in a temperature of say 5°C above freezing. If you add to this a windchill factor and the element of rain, then I would be extremely uncomfortable even with a coat on. Horses can survive outside, but why should they have to just survive?

I do not think that anyone should be ashamed to cosset his or her horse, particularly as he grows old. Why do you think the Government issues cold-weather payments to pensioners? Being cold impairs their health and shortens lives. I believe that the same applies to most mammals, including equines. There are some horses, of course, who will always seem happier outside, but perhaps this is because they have not had good-quality stable care in the past.

Shoeless, Bitless and Disregarding Modern Medicine

There seems to be a growing movement afoot in the UK at present, advocating that the use of horseshoes, bits, saddles and modern medicines is cruel. This, to my mind, is the most ridiculous outlook when applied across the board indiscriminently. I have seen the results of these principles in practice, and believe that it is now causing unnecessary and extreme suffering.Of course there are plenty of horses who can work well without shoes, but this should always be done with the input and advice of a good farrier. Sadly, there are far more horses whose feet and conformation mean that the implementation of this regime causes them crippling pain.

The same goes for saddles. A badly-fitting saddle is to be deplored, but a well-fitting one is a benefit to the horse. Bits are not cruel if fitted and used well, but a bitless bridle can be useful in certain circumstances.

Alternative therapies and natural remedies are wonderful, but there are times when we need to make use of modern veterinary science. Surely, we should endeavour to use the best of the old or natural therapies wherever possible and use modern science where appropriate? The two should go hand in hand.

If most of what we do with our horses were to be considered 'unnatural' (ie the use of bits, saddles, shoes and stabling), then surely riding them would be unnatural too? The ultimate conclusion to this premise would be that we should relinquish ownership and set all our horses free. One of the problems of course would be: where are all the wide open spaces for them to live? Because of thousands of years of domestication, large numbers of them would die horrendous deaths. Obviously this idea is absurd, but I am using this scenario to demonstrate how much suffering can be caused by well-meaning people when a balanced approach is not taken.

Box-Rest or Euthanasia?

I have heard of horses being humanely destroyed because the vet has prescribed six months of box-rest. Sometimes these horses have been relatively young, but the owners have genuinely believed that six months confinement was a fate worse than death and have taken the latter option. I believe that their decisions have been directly affected by the current trend towards 'natural is best'.

Even though I hate the thought of complete box-rest for a horse, on the occasions that I have had need to do this, my horses have settled down to their new routine remarkably well. There are things that can be done to relieve the boredom, which comes with lack of exercise, such as horse toys, a softly-playing radio and ad-lib hay. Probably the best thing for a horse confined to his stable for a long time is human company, preferably that of his 'own human'. They understand when someone really cares for them.

So much is said about the benefits of a 'natural' lifestyle, but little consideration given to the disadvantages, and the suffering that goes on in the wild environment. If a horse becomes badly lame in a wild herd, he is almost bound to die very soon. He cannot keep up with the herd, gets left alone and is set upon by predators. This is perhaps a kinder death than dehydration and starvation, which is the other alternative. The well-loved domesticated horse, on the other hand, has a cosy stable, veterinary treatment, constant food and water, and plenty of attention and sympathy until he recovers, after which he can usually resume an active life again. His only deprivation is a lack of exercise, but the resulting boredom, as I have said, can be greatly minimized. I think many people also underestimate the horse's power of understanding in these situations. They usually do not want to move around too much when they are injured.

The Horse/Human Relationship: Dominance and/or Aggression

Most behaviourists now believe that it is usually a matriarchal mare who actually controls the movement of the herd and is responsible for their safety. She will decide where they eat and drink and when they will leave. She will also keep her herd members in line if they should behave in a dangerous or disruptive manner. In short, it is the matriarchal mare who takes the major burden of responsibility for the well-being of the herd. The stallion will defend his mares from other marauding stallions, but his role in the day-to-day running of herd life is relatively small. This, to my mind, is why mares can often be trickier to deal with and become known as 'mareish'.

'the matriarchal mare controls the herd and is responsible for safety'

Obviously if they are a born leader, it may be difficult at times for them to accept a human leader and, however kind-natured the mare may be, there are often times when she will challenge her handler/trainer for the 'top job'. Often these dominant mares are misunderstood and described as aggressive or nasty, when all they are actually showing are dominant threats. Although it would be unwise to 'call the bluff' of a horse unless we know it extremely well, most of the time these threats are not intended to become attacks. These are situations where we have to tread quite carefully to be just dominant enough in response, without bullying.

Dominance does not have to be aggressive

It is my belief that dominance does not have to go hand in hand with aggression, although it often does so in our society. This is an issue that I feel is greatly misunderstood. The dictionary definition of the word 'dominion' is 'authority to rule'. According to the Old Testament, mankind has been granted a privileged status in our world: a position of dominion over the animal kingdom but one which carries with it great responsibility. The whole of the natural world is our responsibility. If we do not treat it with respect, then we lose it. This is exactly what is happening to the earth today; we are losing species and habitats because of our irresponsibility. The same applies to our animals. They are loaned to us to use and control, but we can only derive the benefits from them if we treat them with respect. Our dominion is a delegated and responsible dominion.

Although the word 'dominion' is not a synonym for 'domination', I feel that the latter has become misinterpreted. The natural world is not ours to do with as we please. We hold it, and all the creatures within, in trust and must manage it responsibly. We are not creating the processes of nature, but should cooperate with them. I believe that within this delegation, we have been given the ability to make minor adjustments, where it is in the best interests of God's creatures for us to do so.

The Native Americans seem to have an almost identical ethos to my interpretation of the Old Testament. They respect every single tree, rock and animal that we are privileged to live alongside. Their attitude to their horses is equally respectful. They have equal status to a member of their family, but at the same time the human is the leader and responsible for the well-being of the horse. The horse, therefore, needs to be disciplined and to have respect for the trainer. Discipline should not be mistaken for aggression or bullying, and it should not be allowed to deteriorate into the latter state. This is the same as the true classical ethos, as laid down by Xenophon 400 years BC. Even though some trainers calling themselves 'classical' have strayed from this path from time to time throughout the years, this is the true philosophy of classical riding which still lives on. Many horses suffer today from a lack of discipline and leadership from humans, as do many riders and trainers. Our horse can still be our best friend, and have respect as well as love for us, as long as our discipline is fair. In addition, we must not neglect to discipline ourselves in all that we do.

It seems to me that some trainers interpret the word 'dominance' to mean 'aggression'. There is one modern trainer who insists that we should aim for a 50/50 relationship with our horse, but that the human is responsible for the situations that the partnership faces. This trainer is insistent that we should not dominate our horses. He seems to infer that dominance equals aggression, and will therefore not entertain the thought that the human should have even a slightly larger balance of power within the partnership. He describes how the balance is constantly shifting from one partner to the other, but that our aim should be to retain the balance as near to 50/50 as possible. While I acknowledge the good intent in this philosophy, I do not think that this is fair to the horse. We should not put this amount of responsibility onto him. I believe that it is our job to be his leader. My favourite way of imagining the horse/human relationship is as so often described by Sylvia Loch: 'Riding should be likened to a dance. The rider is the leader of the dance, but the horse is a willing partner'.

Are Horses Claustrophobic?

Many modern trainers, including Pat Parelli and Richard Maxwell, emphasize the point that horses are born claustrophobic. For a long time, I accepted this premise as it seems feasible; being prey animals that emanate from life on the open plains, horses should be afraid of confined spaces.

However, just lately I have begun to wonder at the validity of applying this claustrophobic 'hat' to all modern horses. The dictionary definition of claustrophobia is 'an abnormal fear of being in an enclosed space'. To me, it would seem perfectly logical that horses should be frightened of being in an enclosed space because they would then be isolated from the herd and therefore vulnerable to predatory attack and unable to utilize their flight instinct. This, surely, makes the horse's fear of an enclosed space completely reasonable and therefore, by definition, not a phobia. To my mind, the fact that most domesticated horses have overcome this fear and are perfectly happy in stables upholds the above assumptions. What is important here is that the domesticated horse has learned to deal with his environment in a rational way.

Another thing that modern 'natural' horsemen constantly tell us, is that horses need freedom. Yes, I heartily agree, one of the most important needs of any horse is freedom from fear. They also, of course, need exercise and freedom from hunger, thirst and pain. Since they are inherently prey animals, fear must be number one on their list of feelings. After the need for sustenance, their need to feel secure is probably the most important thing in their lives and is part of their survival instinct.

Wild horses gain this security from being part of a herd. There is safety in numbers, and they benefit from the best eyes and ears in the herd. As we know, they never all sleep at the same time; there are always horses on watch. The most dangerous place for a horse to be is out in the open on its own. For instance, colts that are nearing maturity and becoming a nuisance to the mares may be driven out of the herd by the matriarchal mare or the herd stallion. These colts will try to band together, but they are still in more danger, being fewer in number, than they would be within the herd. Not only are they at far greater risk from predatory attack, but they find it harder to reach the best grazing and water sources.

'one of the most difficult things we ask our horses to do may be to hack out without other horses'

If a single horse becomes separated from the herd for whatever reason (illness or lameness being two possibilities), it is certainly in mortal danger of becoming easy pickings for a predator. Bearing this in mind, one of the most difficult things that we ask our horses to do may be to hack out without other horses. Should we therefore consider them to be agoraphobic? No. Luckily, most horses are extremely adaptable and trusting souls, and most of them soon learn to look upon their rider as a good herd leader, and put their trust in him.

Things that horses would normally be afraid of, in certain circumstances, can sometimes have the opposite effect. For instance, the rustling of a paper bag while out hacking would frighten my own horse. This is perfectly normal, since the rustling sound is very similar to a predator stalking through the undergrowth. However, the same horse hearing that rustling sound outside the stable, comes rushing to the door with eager anticipation of a tit-bit. Obviously, her instinctual fear of that sound has been overtaken by her pleasant experiences associated with that sound in certain circumstances.

To assume that horses feel 'claustrophobic' all the time that they are in a stable is, to my mind, misguided. They need good stable care, the company of friends, and to be made to feel secure and comfortable. I believe that they do not have abnormal fears. Their fears, on the whole, are completely rational, built upon experience and years of conditioning (considering their inherent instincts). They have learned to overcome their fears, even if their way of rationalizing may be different from our own.

My horses do not travel frequently. The last time I had the need to transport my mare,

I felt very guilty that the trailer seemed so small for her ample dimensions. In fact, when inside, I could only just secure the partition in the central space. When the time came for the return journey, she did not give me a chance to move the partition to widen her entrance. She marched up the ramp so fast I got left behind! She had actually loaded herself; I had not wanted her to go in at that time. She has always travelled very well and hardly moves on the journey. I believe that she uses the padded partition to lean on and therefore feels secure. I have padded the front bar with foam, which also seems to help. I do not think that she is in any way claustrophobic. I suspect that most horses are not; they are merely afraid of strange and unknown things, of which they have no experience and to which they have been unable to develop a logical response.

Loose Schooling

As mentioned previously, in an ideal world, I recognise that it is preferable to allow horses plenty of time each day to socialize, play and relax out in the field. However, I find that there are times when this is not in the horse's best interest. For instance in spring and summer, some horses are literally in mortal danger of eating too much grass, with the risk of colic, laminitis and so on. Starvation paddocks can go some way to solving this problem, but they need to be of a very small size to really stop a good doer from getting too much of the rich short shoots that are likely to grow. This reduction in space can make it impossible for the horse to indulge in a good gallop and buck. In addition, it can be very difficult sometimes in winter conditions to allow the horse enough time and space to let off steam.

I have found that by far the best, and safest, way to let the horse play is to play with him myself. By that I mean a loose-schooling session in an enclosed arena, with a good surface. There are times when the trainer can insist on the horse behaving and doing what is required, even when loose. However, with a good horse/trainer relationship, the horse soon understands when he is being given free licence to go and have fun, and can be actively encouraged to do so by the trainer taking a light-hearted and fun attitude to what he/she is asking the horse to do. I would not advocate this for every horse, as some horses who may have suffered abuse could at first be terrified by this 'freedom'. One has to be tactful and build up a good relationship. My own mare seems to prefer to have a human friend to play with in the arena than to kick up her heels in a muddy field! When the field is muddy, her movements are very slow and deliberate, as if trying to keep her underside area dry.

The Join-Up Technique

Monty Roberts' join-up technique has certainly rocked the world of equestrian training. Some trainers completely dismiss the validity of it, while some use it with discretion. There are other lesser-known trainers not covered in this book who use it indiscriminately. These are the people who, in my opinion, are mainly charlatans and usually have no formal training or in-depth knowledge of the techniques that they are using.

It is fascinating to note the differing opinions of people who have trained with Monty Roberts. Richard Maxwell uses join-up in certain circumstances only, and has slightly adapted the process to suit his own way of helping horses undergoing remedial training.

Kelly Marks appears to use join-up fairly frequently in exactly the same way as Monty Roberts, but advocates its use with caution. She does not recommend its use with all horses, nor that all people should do it. The trainer/handler obviously needs to be well versed in the technique in order to do it well.

Sylvia Loch advises caution over the use of join-up if used on a horse who already has a good relationship with its handler.

All of these approaches seem to me to be valid in their own right. My own opinion lies somewhere in the middle. While I have never felt the need to use join-up with any of my own horses, I would not rule it out in the future if I were to acquire a new horse. However, I feel strongly that it should not be used on very frightened or abused horses, nor on horses who have already bonded with people. Nevertheless, I must reiterate my thoughts on join-up, as expressed in Chapter 7 on Monty Roberts, that it is a wonderful step forward for mankind to be able to communicate with a horse using the horse's own language. For the horses with whom Monty uses this method, it has worked wonders and has been a huge improvement on many of the methods used hitherto.

I think that we should all be very thankful to Monty Roberts for bringing his methods to the fore and making us aware of the horse's body language in a way that the majority of the world perhaps never was before. I say the majority, because I think that there have always been people who did understand the horse's language, for instance the Native Americans. However, to my knowledge, Monty Roberts has made more people aware of it and is the first person to show the world how to communicate with horses using their own language. I believe also that it is largely Monty's methods that have given rise to the vast array of alternative training methods available today, and thus to the production of this book. I hope that I have provoked much discussion and questioning, and that people will always think deeply about the methods that they are using. Hopefully, in this book everyone will find a method or a combination of methods, that prove suitable for themselves and their particular horse.

'I suspect that most horses are not claustrophobic merely afraid of strange and unknown things'

Useful Addresses

Classical Riding Club
Classical Riding Club (CRC), Eden Hall, Kelso,
   Roxburghshire, Scotland, TD5 7QD, UK.
Website: www.classical.riding.co.uk

Doma Vaquera
British Doma Vaquera Association:
   Tel: +44 (0)1234 708626
Doma Vaquera USA: Mary Elizabeth Horan
   Tel. +1 617 527 7477
Doma Vaquera Spain: Joso Fuente Montano
   Tel: +34 954 270611

GaWaNi PONY BOY
Website: www.ponyboy.com

Kelly Marks
Intelligent Horsemanship, Lethornes, Lambourn,
   Berkshire, RG17 8QS, UK.
Tel: +44 (0)1488 71300; Fax :+44 (0)1488 73783
Website: www.intelligenthorsemanship.co.uk

Linda Tellington-Jones
TTeam Headquarters: TTeam and TTouch
   Training, Linda Tellington Jones, PO Box
   3793, Santa Fe, NM 87501, USA.

Tel: +1 505 455 2945 or +1 800 854 TEAM
Fax: +1 505 455 7233
Email: tteam@compuserve.com
TTeam-UK: Sarah Fisher, South Hill House,
Radford, Bath BA3 1QQ, UK.
Tel: +44 (0)1761 471182
Fax: +44 (0)1761 472982
Email: sarahfisher@msn.com

Monty Roberts
Email: kelly@montyroberts.co.uk
Website: www.montyroberts.com

Parelli Natural Horsemanship
Email: info@parelliuk.com; pnhusa@parelli.com
Websites: www.parelli.biz; www.parelli.com
   www.parellinaturalhorsemanship.com;

The Feldenkrais Method
Feldenkrais International Training Centre
PO Box 1207, Hove, East Sussex BN3 2GG
Tel: +44 (0) 1273 327406
Fax: +44 (0) 1273 725299
Websites: www.feldenkrais-itc.org;
www.feldenkrais.co.uk
Email: enquiries@feldenkrais.co.uk

Further Reading and Bibliography

Belasik, Paul *Dressage for the 21st Century* (JA
   Allen) 2002
Decarpentry, General Albert *Academic
   Equitation* (JA Allen) 1971
De la Guérinière, Francois Robichon *Ecole de
   Cavalierie*, Paris 1733; Translated as *Schools
   of Horsemanship* (JA Allen) 1994
GaWaNi PONY BOY *Horse Follow Closely*
   (BowTie Press) 1998
——*Of Women and Horses* (BowTie Press) 2000
——*Out of the Saddle* (BowTie Press) 1998
——*Time Well Spent* (BowTie Press) 1998
——*Native American Horsemanship, Step by
   Step* (Kosmos Verlag) 2002
——*My Horse Series*, Limited Edition (Pony
   Boy Press) 2003
Hartley Edwards, Elwyn *Saddlery* (JA Allen)
   1963
Loch, Sylvia *The Royal Horse of Europe* (JA
   Allen) 1986
——*The Classical Seat* (A Horse & Rider

   Publication) 1988
——*Dressage* (Sportsmans Press) 1990
——*The Classical Rider* (JA Allen) 1997
——*Dressage in Lightness* (JA Allen) 2000
——*Invisible Riding* (DJ Murphy (Publishers)
   Ltd.) 2003
Marks, Kelly *Perfect Manners – How to Behave
   so Your Horse Does Too* (Ebury Press) 2002
——*Creating a Bond with Your Horse*
   (Intelligent Horsemanship booklet)
——*Leading and Loading* (Intelligent
   Horsemanship booklet)
——*Handling the Untouched Horse* (Intelligent
   Horsemanship booklet)
——*Catching Horses Made Easy* (Intelligent
   Horsemanship booklet)
McBane, Susan and Davis, Caroline
   *Complementary Therapies for Horse and
   Rider* (David & Charles Ltd) 2001
——*100 Ways to Improve Your Riding* (David
   & Charles Ltd) 2004

Maxwell, Richard and Bayley, Lesley *Understanding Your Horse* (David & Charles Ltd) 1996
——*From Birth to Backing* (David & Charles Ltd) 2001
——and Sharples, Johanna *Unlock Your Horse's Talent* (David & Charles Ltd) 2003
Oliveira, Nuño *Classical Principles of the Art of Training Horses* (Howley & Russell, Australia) 1983
Parelli, Pat *Natural Horsemanship* (Western Horseman Inc) 1993
Podhajsky, Col. Alois *The Complete Training of Horse & Rider* (George G. Harrap & Co. Ltd) 1967
Roberts, Monty *The Man Who Listens to Horses* (Random House Press) 1986
——*Shy Boy – The Horse Who Came in from the Wild* (Harper Collins) 1999
——*Join Up – Horse Sense for Humans* (Harper Collins) 2000
——*From My Hands to Yours* (Published by Monty Roberts) 2002
Seunig, Waldemar *Horsemanship* (Doubleday) 1974; Translated from German by Robert Hale & Co. 1976

Stanier, Sylvia *The Art of Long Reining* (Robert Hale) 1972
——*The Art of Lungeing* (Robert Hale) 1976
——*Mrs. Houblon's Side Saddle* by Mrs. Archer Houblon, Revised, up-dated and published by Sylvia Stanier 1986
——*Classical Circus Equitation* (The Works of HJ Lijsen) Edited, described, explained and published by Sylvia Stanier 1993
(All Sylvia Stanier's books are available directly from the author: Tel: +44 (0)1604 686221)
Tellington-Jones, Linda and Bruns, Ursula *An Introduction to the Tellington-Jones Equine Awareness Method* (Breakthrough Publications Inc.) 1985
——and Taylor, Sybil *The Tellington Touch* (Cloudcraft Books) 1992
——and Taylor, Sybil *Getting in Touch with Horses* (Kenilworth Press) 1995
——and Pabel, Andrea *Let's Ride with Linda Tellington-Jones* (Kenilworth Press) 1997
——*Improve Your Horse's Wellbeing – A step by step guide to TTouch and TTeam Training* (Kenilworth Press) 1999
Xenophon *The Art of Horsemanship* (JA Allen) 1962 (Original publication approx. 400BC)

Videos

Sylvia Loch
The Classical Seat I
The Classical Seat II
The Classical Seat III
On the Bit
Perfect Laterals – Shoulder-In
Perfect Laterals – Travers towards Half Pass
Staying On
(All of Sylvia's books and videos are available in most book shops or on the Internet at www.classical-dressage.net)

GaWaNi PONY BOY
GaWaNi PONY BOY *Horse Follow Closely* Video Set (BowTie Press) 1999

Parelli Natural Horsemanship
The Future of Training – Eventing
Riding with Fluidity by Linda Parelli
The Art of Freestyle Riding
Teaching Your Horse at Liberty

Leads & Lead Changes
A Natural Beginning
Do More with Your Horse…Naturally
Discover the Secrets to Success with Horses
National Geopgraphic – Lost Mustang Story
The 7 Games of Natural Horsemanship
Understanding Natural Horsemanship (Audio)

Monty Roberts
Join-Up
Fix-Up 1 – Crossing Water/Head Shy/Pull Back
Fix-Up 2 – Veterinarian/Loader/Mounting/Kicking Rings
Fix-Up 3 – Preparing for Farrier
How to Use A Dually Halter
Follow-Up, Days One to Four (three videos set)
Shy Boy – The Horse Who Came in From The Wild
(All of Monty Roberts's and Kelly Marks's books and videos are available from Kelly Marks at Intelligent Horsemanship – see above)

Index